Christopher Ward

Our cheque is in the post

illustrated by Frank Dickens

Pan Books in association with
Secker and Warburg

First published 1980 by Martin Secker and Warburg Ltd
This edition published 1982 by Pan Books Ltd,
Cavaye Place, London SW10 9PG
in association with Martin Secker and Warburg Ltd
text © Christopher Ward 1980
illustrations © Frank Dickens 1980
ISBN 0 330 26657 8
Printed and bound in Great Britain by
Richard Clay (The Chaucer Press) Ltd, Bungay, Suffolk

Our cheque is in the post

Christopher Ward is the author of *How to Complain*. He is an Assistant Editor of the *Daily Mirror* and writes a weekly humorous column which is syndicated world wide. Frank Dickens is one of Britain's most popular cartoonists, best known for his 'Bristow' strip cartoon which appears in newspapers and magazines all over the world.

Also by Christopher Ward
in Pan Books

How to Complain

INDEX of Excuses

LETTERS to my publishers

May 25th, 1977

Dear Mr Secker and Mr Warburg,
Thank you for your kind letter reminding me about the delivery date of *Our Cheque Is in the Post*.

After two years' hard writing I am pleased to be able to confirm that I have indeed completed the manuscript but, unhappily, at the very last minute fate has intervened most cruelly, with tragic consequences.

Yesterday afternoon I placed the completed typescript on my desk while I went downstairs to the telephone to make arrangements to have the pages photocopied, as is stipulated in our contract. Because of the warm weather we have been enjoying of late I had (you may think foolishly) left the window of my study fully open. Unknown to me, while I was on the telephone, my wife opened the back door to hang out the washing, occasioning a violent draught to sweep through the house, carrying into the street every page of my manuscript except the last, which I enclose herewith.

Doubtless you will have read in the newspapers about the Clean Up London campaign whose admirable aim is to clear our streets of rubbish. It was my further misfortune that this very afternoon my road was the thoroughfare singled out by the organisers for their attention. By the time I returned to my desk, the campaign's refuse collectors had committed every last sweet paper, ice-lolly stick, and closely typed sheet of paper in the street to its mobile incinerator.

But let me not dwell on past events, especially such unhappy ones. The important thing now, I'm sure you will agree, is to reassemble my notes and start again at the beginning so that you will be able to publish the book if not this Christmas, at least *next* Christmas.

As publishers with a reputation of sensitivity towards their authors' feelings, you will understand what a savage blow the events of yesterday were to my morale and I know that you would not want to add to my burden by making me suffer financially, too. I wondered therefore if you would consider advancing me a further £2,000 subsidy for this unforeseen and unavoidable additional year of work.

Yours, etc.

June 1st, 1977

Dear Mr Secker and Mr Warburg,

Thank you for your understanding note and for the cheque for £2,000. You can rely upon me to deliver the completed manuscript on or before June 1st, 1978, and rest assured that it will be even better than the first, which you sadly never had the opportunity to read. And *this* time I'll take a carbon copy, as you suggest!

Yours, etc.

October 10th, 1978

Dear Mr Secker and Mr Warburg,

Thank you for your letters of September 12th, 26th, 30th, October 3rd, 5th, and, finally, your recorded delivery letter dated yesterday.

There is no point in trying to conceal from you the

fact that I have been avoiding you and I humbly apologise for neither replying to your letters nor returning your many telephone calls. The truth of the matter is, I have been anxiously waiting to hear from the British Rail lost property office at Victoria about the whereabouts of my completed manuscript of *Our Cheque Is in the Post*.

You probably read earlier this month in the *Daily Telegraph* about the awful business of that pregnant teenaged girl throwing herself under a train at East Grinstead station. Well, I had the misfortune to be one of the passengers waiting on the platform at the time of the tragedy, and took part in the subsequent fruitless attempts to lift the guard's van off the poor girl's legs before the fire brigade arrived.

When it became clear that nothing more could be done, and after giving my address to the police, I then boarded a train for London to deliver the manuscript to you. Unfortunately, because of the distressed state I was in, I left behind in the waiting room my briefcase containing not only the finished manuscript but also the carbon copy I had taken as a precaution against loss.

I reported my loss to the station master as soon as I arrived at Victoria, and also informed the Railway Police, but I regret to tell you that, so far, my briefcase has not been handed in. Believe me, I now know the depths of despair to which T. E. Lawrence must have sunk when he mislaid *The Seven Pillars of Wisdom* in less extenuating circumstances.

I have today placed an advertisement in *The Times* offering a reward of £5,000 for the safe return of my manuscript and I hope this will produce results. It should, anyway, impress on you my determination to deliver this manuscript into your hands at the earliest possible moment. If, however, the typescript for some reason does not turn up, it would be quite wrong of me to deceive you as to the gravity of the loss, since the briefcase also contained *all* of my notes, research material, and reference material for the book. As I would have to start from scratch, we would be talking of delivery of the new manuscript no earlier than, say, March 1979.

Yours, etc.

October 12th, 1978

Dear Mr Secker and Mr Warburg,

Thank you for your understanding letter and for your cheque for £1,000, which will certainly tide me over. You're quite right, of course, it would be wrong to hang around indefinitely hoping that the darned thing will turn up when, for all I know, it might be lost for ever. I have therefore taken your advice and started work on the project as from today and am aiming at delivery by March 1st, 1980.

Yours, etc.

March 1st, 1980

Dear Mr Secker and Mr Warburg,

I make it a rule never to inflict my personal problems upon anyone for whom I work because I have always regarded it as unprofessional to let one's private life intrude in any way on one's working commitments. But I regret that the deteriorating condition of my crippled brother Herbert has compelled me on this occasion to reconsider my principles.

Briefly, Herbert was born with parafibramotosis and, since early childhood, has undergone a series of major operations in the hope that one day he may be able to walk. In January the doctors fitted him with a bionic spine, but the operation was not a total success and, since the tragic death of his wife last year, the onus of looking after him has fallen largely on me, the only surviving relative.

The assistance and comfort I have been able to provide has been largely at the expense of the book, I'm afraid. I realise that your schedules are getting very tight for this Christmas, but is there any chance of, say, a three-month extension of the deadline? I ask this not so much for myself but for Herbert.

Yours, etc.

March 4th, 1980

Dear Mr Secker and Mr Warburg,

Thank you for your understanding letter. I'm not surprised that you didn't know I have a brother. He doesn't get about much and I try not to mention him because of the pain his tragic circumstances cause me when I think about him. I'm most grateful, anyway, for the three-month extension. No, of course I won't let you down. Have I ever? At least, unlike some of your other authors, not without a perfectly good reason.

Yours, etc.

CHRISTOPHER WARD

WHAT is an Excuse?

Excuses: where would we be without them? Right up to our necks in it, that's where. Excuses don't just get us off the hook – they make others feel better about our failures. We owe it to the people we let down never to let them discover the truth.

What is an excuse? The dictionary defines it as 'an explanation offered in defence . . .' Just how powerful and effective a defence depends largely on your inventiveness.

A successful excuse must achieve one of three objectives:

RELEASE you from an obligation to do something you ought to do but can't or don't want to.

CLEAR you of all blame for some failure for which you may or may not be responsible (but probably are).

PROVIDE a convincing explanation as to why you didn't do something that someone else would have liked you to do.

The right excuse, delivered in the correct manner, must leave the other person so convinced of your frustration and disappointment that they will share in it and feel guilty for being a party to your misfortune.

But the best excuse is not necessarily the true one. The Post Office, public transport, mechanical breakdowns, and traffic jams have all been totally devalued as excuses by use and abuse. At best they are incapable of arousing sympathy, at worst they are simply not believed.

It could be that your car has indeed broken down on the way to an important appointment, for instance, but will this explanation be accepted as the truth by the person whom you have kept waiting? And even if it is, will the other person perhaps take the view that you should have taken adequate precautions against such a commonplace event? You would be doing yourself and everyone else a favour if you attributed your delay to a bank hold-up, a suicide attempt by your neighbour, or an encounter with a crazed baboon fleeing a private safari park.

Similarly, your genuine reasons for, say, not accepting an invitation to a party may be insulting to the friends who hoped to entertain you. For the sake of their self-esteem, you ought to find more compelling competition for their night of mystery and magic than a burning need to spend the evening at home with your feet up in front of the telly.

On the following pages I will be outlining some of the alternatives open to you in every field of failure, but it would be nice to think that you will use this book in a creative way to build for yourself a whole new life of deceit. A good excuse is your social parachute. Don't be afraid to pull the rip-cord!

ANIMALS, excuses for barring friends' (*See also* **Children**, excluding from invitations) Other people's pets are a big enough pain in their own home without having them inflicted on you in yours, so when friends announce that they will be arriving accompanied, immediate preventative action has to be taken.

Saying, 'We'd love to see you but not your poofy poodle' is tantamount to telling your friends not to bring a husband or wife. They will take strong exception to your request, and rightly so. What you have to do is find an excuse that will make them *want* to leave their horrible little four-footed friend behind.

A killer mink on the loose works a treat in the country, I always find. Emphasise the death toll ('four dogs already this week, *and* the vicar's cat') and the unpleasant method of sudden death meted out. ('Minks always disembowel their prey. Horrible!')

A trigger-happy local farmer whose sheep have been worried by stray dogs is also an effective deterrent. ('He never misses – got a Cruft's winner last year.')

In town, the presence of a neurotic animal belonging to another visitor is an acceptable excuse for barring friends' pets – it demonstrates, after all, that you are acting in the best interests of animals and not just imposing your prejudices on others. An aunt visiting with her easily frightened chihuahua, perhaps? Or if your guests are themselves intending to bring a chihuahua, an uncle visiting with his Dobermann will do the trick. The absence of the alibi pet when your guests arrive can be easily explained by a last-minute change in plans.

There's no reason why you or a member of your family shouldn't develop a violent allergy to the fur of domestic animals. ('I'd love you to bring Shandy, but honestly I simply dare not have him in the house. The doctor says that if . . .')

The convenience of allergies is that they can go away as quickly and mysteriously as they afflict you and they make a good talking point when your friends arrive dog-less. ('Last time I stroked a cat I came out in blotches and sneezed for a week.')

APPOINTMENTS, excuses for not making

The polite response to the statement, 'We must have lunch some time' is 'Yes, we must.' If the first speaker has any sensitivity at all, the conversation should end there and the subject of lunch never be mentioned again unless the other person brings it up.

But determined would-be hosts won't let it go at that. They will try to bully you into committing yourself to a date, a time, and a place. If you don't find an excuse immediately for not being able to name the day, you'll only have to extricate yourself from the arrangement at a later date, with the certain risk of another appointment being fixed.

In these circumstances, the answer to the question, 'When are you free?' is: 'I'll have to have a look in my master diary which unfortunately I don't have with me at the moment.' It's not difficult never to be in the same place as this fictional 'master diary', which is not to be confused with your desk diary or even your pocket diary.

Deaths and illness are not convincing reasons for not fixing advance appointments, unless they are genuine and can be corroborated. On the other hand, the death of a distant aunt who has named you as executor of her will is likely to leave you extremely busy for a number of weeks.

Another handy get-out is one much favoured by

members of the Royal Family, who from time to time announce that they have 'cancelled all engagements until further notice'. There could be any number of good reasons for a self-imposed withdrawal from social life for you, too. What about an extreme hardship diet that doesn't even permit you a lettuce leaf or a glass of water? Writers are forever telling people, 'Forgive me, but I'm not making any arrangements until I've finished this blasted book I'm working on.' There is no blasted book, of course, but no one ever knows.

The demands of organising the Parents' Association May Day carnival could equally necessitate a temporary retreat. 'I'd hate to have to cancel you – let's fix something when I've got my head above water' will be so appreciated for its brutal honesty that no one will realise you're lying.

ATTEND, inability to   An invitation, it says here, is 'an offer of hospitality or entertainment'. If you decline to accept such warm-hearted generosity you will certainly disappoint your expectant host or hostess and may even nark them. Unless, that is, you have a good reason for *not* being able to attend.

There can be only three main grounds for refusal, besides the true one of not wanting to go, of course.

1   Geographical – i.e., you are here and they are there and, due to insurmountable transport difficulties, you physically cannot transport yourself from A to B and back again.

2   You have previously committed yourself to doing something else at the same time and cannot extricate yourself from the arrangement.

3   Unavoidable circumstances and other factors that would equally prevent you going to collect a

cheque for a pools win of £500,000 on the same day, at the same time, in the same place.

All three are rich in possibilities for the social escapologist.

Travel difficulties

There is a condition known as nyctalopia – in layman's terms, night blindness – which makes it dangerous, if not impossible, to drive a car at night. It is a condition which is certainly worth cultivating for friends who are inaccessible by public transport.

Broken-down cars are no excuse unless the cause of the breakdown is an interesting or unusual one. 'Some kids in the street stuffed Play-doh up my exhaust and the engine did a Mount St Helens when I was doing 90 mph down the fast lane of the M5' is an OK excuse, on account of the fact that it will provide a talking point for your rejected host and hostess in your absence.

It is perfectly reasonable to refuse to travel by public transport at night, or even during the day, if you have ever been mugged. It's worth putting this about, in case you ever need to use the excuse. No one can fail to sympathise with a guest whose polite refusal starts, '*Ever since I was mugged . . .*'

Previous engagement

This must be less glamorous than the one you are turning down, and you should make your insistence on going ahead with this previous arrangement a public demonstration of your absolute and unassailable integrity. Like the surgeon's wife who told friends: 'I'm afraid we can't come to dinner. My husband's been lucky enough to obtain a corpse and wants to practise a new operation.'

Phrase your excuse more tactfully than Oscar Wilde, who said: 'Unfortunately I have a subsequent engagement.'

Unavoidable circumstances

If your popularity rating is twenty-one out of a possible score of twenty, it will soon plummet to zero when you inform people your doctor thinks you might have hepatitis.

'Our baby-sitter has just discovered she is pregnant' offers no clue as to why you should be prevented from attending a dinner in three weeks' time, but it carries an authoritative air of crisis about it. Maybe that's the day you're taking her in for an abortion? Maybe you can't find another baby-sitter because word has gone round the neighbourhood that you're the one who got her into trouble? It leaves people wondering, but not about your inability to attend.

'Thank you, but we never do' has a finality that cannot be disputed when offered as a reason for not spending a weekend with friends.

So does, 'I've had a psychic premonition . . .'

'Unfortunately my wife's father's body is being exhumed on that day' invites the question 'Why?' to which the answer is, 'We have no idea, it's all very worrying.' You are immediately excused *everything*.

The best reason of all for not visiting someone's home is a point-blank refusal to leave your own. The explanation here is: 'We're expecting burglars', delivered in the same tone as you might announce, 'We've got the in-laws staying.' Housebreakers, when foiled in their first attempt to gain entry, often return for a second crack and no one would expect you to lose the colour telly and the wife's jewels for the sake of their bring-and-buy or a barbecue.

The *shortest* excuse is a telegram, which says simply: 'Diarrhoea. Writing.'

BED, excuses for being caught in (with someone you shouldn't be there with) The late
Henry Miller told the story of how one of his wives set
out to catch him *in flagrante delicto* by returning early
from holiday. She found him in bed with her best
friend.

'What did you do?' asked a BBC interviewer.

'I left my wife immediately, of course,' said Miller.
'I couldn't tolerate being married to a woman who
didn't trust me.'

If he hadn't been a man of integrity and principles,
of course, Miller could have saved his marriage.
When Mrs Miller walked in, he could have said:
'Before you jump to any conclusions, my dear, wait
until you have spoken to the private detective who is
going to walk through that door in exactly three
minutes' time carrying a camera. April and her
husband want to rush their divorce through and I
agreed to help them by providing evidence of
adultery. But no one must know that nothing of a
sexual nature transpired between April and me
otherwise the divorce would be declared null and void
on the grounds of collusion. And, don't worry, my
dear, my name *won't* be brought into it.'

Ten minutes later, when no private detective has
appeared, Miller would have said: 'I'm afraid my
wife's untimely arrival may have frightened away our
private eye, April. After all, he stands to lose his
licence if anyone finds out it's a put-up job. I suggest
we try again tomorrow.

'Is that all right with you, dear? By the way, how
was your holiday? Tell me all about it while April is
getting dressed . . .'

There can be only one other legitimate reason why
you are apparently engaged in an act of shameless
adultery. You are on a mission of mercy. Your partner
is a terminal cancer patient with one week to live, who

has made one last request: you. It meant nothing. It would have been churlish to deny a dying person one last moment of sexual gratification. The fact that your extra-marital partner is so attractive makes the situation all the more tragic that, this time next week, they'll be pushing up the daisies.

Chico Marx, caught kissing a chorus girl, told Mrs Marx: 'I wasn't kissing her. I was whispering in her mouth.'

BILLS, non-payment of   Assuming that you don't dispute that you owe the money for services rendered or goods supplied, there can be only three plausible explanations for a bill not being settled:

(a) you never received it
(b) something happened to it after you received it but before you could pay it
(c) you paid it but they never received your money.

All three reasons for non-payment have one thing in common: they are not your fault.

Why did you never receive it?

No, it wasn't lost in the post. Nor was it sent to the wrong address. It wasn't even destroyed in a fire at your local sorting office. *It was stolen by the postman.* Why should your postman wish to steal a plumber's bill for £19.60, plus VAT? Because he couldn't cope, that's why. Unable to complete his round in the time available, he started taking mail home with him, with the intention of delivering it the following day. Alas, next day . . .

By the time Post Office investigators caught up with him, his three-bedroomed semi was crammed with more than eight thousand sacks of undelivered letters, one of which contained – you can only presume – the unpaid plumber's bill.

The Post Office are working flat out to deliver the

stolen mail, some of it dating back eleven years, and as soon as they have cleared the backlog, you will settle the account. You'd like to settle it before, but some of the undelivered letters contain cheques payable to you and without these funds you cannot meet your present commitments.

What happened to it after you received it but before you could pay it?

Your green Amazon parrot ate it. Unfortunately the shredded pieces of paper at the bottom of his cage were too few and too small to be able to determine the nature of the document, and you are most grateful to them for making it possible to identify it. Regrettably, your parrot also ate a cheque payable to you and you will be unable to settle this account until a new cheque has been drawn in your favour.

How come you paid it but they never received your money?

As you were ill in bed with 'flu at the time you wrote the cheque, you gave the letter to the window cleaner to post. Shortly after leaving your house, but before he had posted your letter containing the cheque, your window cleaner was arrested while placing his ladder against a wall by the window of the dormitory of a girls' school. As a known offender, he was refused bail and subsequently sentenced to nine months' imprisonment. Only then was your letter discovered among his effects and returned to you by the Governor of Pentonville Prison.

BORES, excuses for escaping from Bores are, by their very nature, insensitive people, which is why they are so blissfully unaware of the paralysing effect they have on others. Fortunately, their lack of sensitivity makes them relatively easy to escape from without hurting their feelings.

Offer to top up the bore's drink and make a beeline with his/her glass for the bar. Bores are accustomed to being deserted in mid-drink, for reasons they have never been able to fathom, so your offer will immediately be mistaken for a friendly gesture. It is no such thing, of course. On the way to the bar, find a sympathetic friend and ask them to rescue you. ('Oh, Henry, there's someone I want you to meet. Please excuse us a moment, will you?') The bore will wander off to find a new victim.

In the absence of a friend, bung the barman or waiter a quid and tell him that in exactly three minutes' time you want him to call you away to a non-existent telephone call, or inquire if you are the owner of the green and white Marina estate car.

In the absence of a friend or a friendly barman, spill your drink down yourself and rush off to the bathroom to sponge yourself down.

At a lunch or dinner party

Sciatica is a painful affliction, as any sufferer will tell you, but in your case it has imposed upon you the

additional handicap of being unable to turn your head or body to the left (if the bore is sitting on your left) or the right (if the bore is sitting on your right). 'I'm afraid I can't hear a thing out of this ear' is also a good conversation-stopper.

On a train or plane journey

Moving to another seat is the best solution, but not always possible. The only other alternatives are the fairly brutal ones of going to sleep ('Will you forgive me for nodding off – I've got a busy schedule ahead and two nights' lost sleep to catch up on?') or burying your head in a book or paperwork ('You're going to think me terribly rude, but I've had to set aside the entire journey to catch up on my reading. What a pity, because I would have enjoyed a natter . . .').

On holidays

There is no longer-lasting bore than the holiday bore. Prevention is better than cure: a stubborn refusal to be drawn into conversation, a polite rejection of all offers of hospitality. But to determined bores, even unfriendliness is no deterrent. You need a good lie.

For couples: Your holiday is a last-ditch attempt to save your marriage/love affair which is in trouble due to too much socialising back home. You have come away 'to find each other again'.

For singles: For reasons not entirely unconnected with national security, you have come away on your own because you 'need time to think'. Your problem is one you can share with no one.

CANCELLING a business date or social engagement With the exception of 'I'm leaving you', the announcement 'I'm terribly sorry but I can't make it' is probably the most difficult about-turn that we ever have to spring on another person. Even if the friend or acquaintance is secretly relieved that we are standing them up, they will still be asking themselves who is more entertaining or more important to us than they are. The onus is on us to convince them that this change of plans has been imposed on us by duty or disaster.

The best reason for being here (where you want to be) and not there (where they expect you to be) is that you cannot leave the telephone even for ten minutes. This is because you are awaiting a call from the hospital 'to hear how the operation went'.

If you have a very high-powered job a business deal involving many thousands of dollars, requiring an instant decision by you, could also transform you into a telephone slave. With so much at stake you can't risk confusing the caller by notifying him at this late stage that you will be at a different number from seven until ten, and thereafter at the original number, etc. Besides, as everyone knows, these calls have a habit of coming through when you are travelling between telephone A and telephone B.

Being burgled is a good reason for breaking an engagement, but *suspecting* that you have been burgled is even better, because there's less chance of the lie being found out later.

The story goes like this: You have arrived home and discovered evidence that someone has broken into your home, although nothing appears to be missing. Nevertheless you call the police who insist that, for your own protection and for insurance reasons, you draw up a complete inventory of all your possessions. It's the only way, they say, of discovering now – instead of in six months' time – that your silver christening mug has vanished. You are now going through every drawer, cupboard, and shelf in the house.

The beauty of this excuse is that when your friends visit your home two weeks later and find everything exactly as it was, they won't sit there wondering whether the burglary was a cock-and-bull story you invented to get out of attending their boring silver wedding party.

The many misfortunes that can befall a home provide you with a veritable mine of misinformation.

Lightning strikes are far more common than is generally thought, one consequence of them being that you have to stay in to meet the borough surveyor, your own architect, the local builder, and the insurance assessor, all of whom are calling to inspect the damage.

Illness – unless serious, prolonged, *and* genuine – doesn't wash as a reason for extricating yourself from an engagement; but injury does. The most convincing 'can't make it' excuse I've ever been given came from a friend who telephoned to say she had been struck on the shoulder by a piece of metal that fell out of the sky. No, she hadn't been hurt – a convincing touch, that – but the incident had been witnessed by a policeman who formed the view that the missile could only have fallen from an airliner passing many thousands of feet overhead. The reason my friend couldn't keep our date was that an aircraft investigator from Farnborough was calling on her that evening to examine the fragment and question her about the circumstances of the accident. The lie had the unmistakable ring of truth about it.

Funerals, like illness, have been done to death so to speak and should be avoided at all costs unless you can make them interesting. The funeral of an aunt is an unacceptable reason for cancelling a previous engagement, even if it's true, because no one will believe you. 'The funeral of my father's mistress for thirty-five years', on the other hand, will excite your audience's curiosity and win their sympathy.

Public duty intervenes at the most convenient moments, in the form of jury service or being called as a witness at an inquest ('Why me? I mean, I hardly even *saw* the accident'). Both have a thoroughly authoritative air of compulsion about them.

Finally, the most cancelled social engagement of them all, the business lunch. I doubt if half the lunches that are fixed, then carefully noted in mutual diaries, ever take place. By being called off they cause more ill-will than the goodwill they were intended to engender. Unless, that is, you have an excuse that the other person can understand and identify with.

There is only one such excuse in business-lunch circles: crawling. A last-minute invitation by a superior or, better still, by the chairman, editor, or chief executive, is a very good reason to call off lunch with anyone else. They'd do it to you and they don't mind you doing it to them, just so long as you level with them by playing down the 'important meeting' aspect of the invitation, which sounds dreadfully pompous, and emphasise the opportunities it offers to ingratiate yourself.

But when you then take out the busty blonde from Accounts, don't take her anywhere you're likely to bump into the businessman you have just stood up.

CAR, crashing a   I am indebted to a van driver from Arlingsaas in the far north of Sweden for the most original successful excuse ever advanced for crashing a car. '*I couldn't see where I was going, officer,*' he said. '*The windscreen was completely fogged up by the heavy breathing of all those mice.*'

The driver was a mouse-breeder on his way, one frosty morning, to a research laboratory with five cages of the little rodents when his van plunged off the road.

Other drivers' explanations are less convincing and serve only to amuse the police, who take the statements, and insurance assessors, who read the claim forms. Here are a few worth steering clear of. They all have one thing in common: it was the other driver's fault.

The accident was due to the other fellow narrowly missing me.

I knocked over the man; he admitted it was his fault as he had been knocked down before.

I misjudged a lady crossing the road.

I collided with a stationary tree.

Coming back, I took the wrong turning and drove into a tree that was not there.

I thought the side window was down, but it was up, as I found when I pushed my head through it.

I was keeping two yards from each lamp post, which were in a straight line. Unfortunately there was a bend in the road, bringing a right-hand lamp post in line with the other and of course I landed in the river.

To avoid a collision I ran into the other lorry.

My accident was due to the road bending.

Whilst waiting at traffic lights, I was rammed by the stationary car behind me.

I was having a dispute with my wife. She pulled my hair, causing me to turn into a lamp standard.

The other man turned into a coal sack.

Coming home, I drove into the wrong house and collided with a tree I haven't got.

A pedestrian hit me and went under my car.

I leaned forward to swat a fly on the windscreen and hit the car in front.

In my limited experience of crashing cars, I have found that just two words work an absolute treat:

'Bloody dogs!' Since there was no dog, this inevitably provokes the question from eye-witnesses, 'What dog?' to which you reply: 'The bloody great Alsatian that ran straight out in front of me. I'm not surprised you didn't see it. I hardly saw it myself, it was going so damned fast.'

Within five minutes, providing you give a good performance and spend some time on your knees searching for dog hairs in your front bumper, you will have three eye-witnesses who will swear they saw you swerve or brake to avoid a dog, and one of them will even know whose dog it was. The dog, fortunately, won't be able to deny it. Meanwhile you can point to the crumpled wreck of your car, presenting yourself as the great animal lover who occasioned this expensive damage rather than see a stray die beneath your wheels or be maimed for life.

The circumstances of some crashes do not lend themselves to the dashing Alsatian excuse. On these occasions you must place the blame jointly on the designer of your vehicle and the manufacturers of your shoes. Together they loused it up because your right foot *became jammed between the accelerator and the brake.*

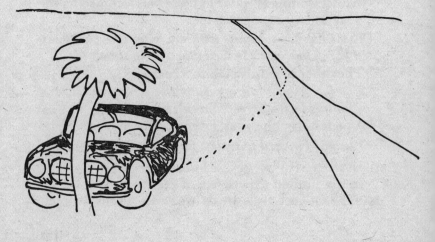

CHARITY, not giving to (*See also* **Whip-rounds**, not being blackmailed into) Nobody likes to be thought tight-fisted, especially if they are. When you decline to make a contribution to a charity, however undeserving the cause, the immediate assumption is that your motive is one of meanness, even if you offer to submit yourself to a body search in the middle of Oxford Circus to prove that you don't have a halfpenny on you.

No, the reason you cannot, *will not*, give must be founded on the highest principles and you should spell these out to the lady flogging flags: 'Thank you for giving me the opportunity to contribute to your cause but I make it a rule never to support private charities because any donation – however small – would merely encourage the State to evade its responsibilities.'

There is a less tactful response to doorstep appeals by religious sects which will enable you to dispose of your caller without burning the toast. The conversation, brief and to the point, should go like this:

'Good morning. We are Jehovah's Witnesses and . . .'

'And you have been collecting money for your worthy cause and you would like to talk to me about it.'

'Yes, we . . .'

'I can't tell you how glad I am that you called. You see, I'm Jehovah. How much have we made so far today?'

CHILDREN, excluding from invitations (*See also* **Animals**, barring friends') Other people's children, like other people's pets, can be pests, but you can't expect the parents to share this point of view. Therefore excluding children without driving their parents away, too, requires skill, diplomacy, and ruthless cynicism.

For hosts and hostesses with children themselves, the standard ploy used to be to announce the presence in the home of an infectious illness such as measles or mumps. But trendy parents have rather short-circuited this one by announcing, 'Oh, that's good, we're very anxious that Justin should catch it and get it out of the way once and for all.'

No one is queueing up to catch gastric 'flu, on the other hand, because no parent relishes the prospect of escorting their child to and from the loo at twenty-minute intervals for three consecutive nights. When your guests arrive childless, however, you should keep your own children out of the way – ostensibly to prevent them passing on gastric 'flu to your guests, but in reality to minimise the chances of them revealing that they are enjoying perfect health.

The child-free host and hostess have to find a different, no less compelling reason to keep other people's kids away. 'We're having some electrical work done in the house and the contractors have knocked off for the weekend leaving bare wires at child level' is an invitation to your friends to watch their children being plugged in to 240 volts AC. To corroborate your story you only have to poke some cable through a couple of holes in the floorboards or out of a gap under the skirting, leaving the stripped wires dangling menacingly at strategic points around the house. No one is going to touch the wires to find out whether or not they're connected to the mains.

Another line of defence is to organise some activity that no one would wish their children to be exposed to: a blue movie after lunch, perhaps; the promise of an exotic joint or hash cake. ('For the children's sake, perhaps it would be better . . .')

My final suggestion is a rather wicked one, but its

effectiveness puts it in the black plague league. All you need to say is, 'You *will* bring Damian, won't you, because we've got someone coming who is just going to *love* him. He's terribly gay and – so the story goes – a convicted child-molester, but we've never been convinced of his guilt because, frankly, he's so terribly amusing.'

When your friends arrive without the horrible little Damian, you tell them: 'How right you were not to bring him. Our friend won't be here today because the police picked him up last night approaching a small boy at Fenchurch Street public conveniences.'

CONTROL, circumstances beyond our

This is the standard excuse much favoured by large organisations, such as British Rail, and small disorganisations, such as builders. It is trotted out to explain away a multiplicity of sins and omissions and carries with it heavy implications of a series of Acts of God and Acts of Ayatollas. It is understood by everybody on the receiving end to mean, 'I cocked it up and haven't even got the wit or imagination to dream up a convincing excuse.'

For this reason, Circumstances Beyond Our Control should not be in your arsenal of excuses, except as an act of revenge on those who use it on us. In this context it can be highly effective at stalling the professional self-excusers. For instance:

Dear Sir,

Thank you for your letter concerning the unpaid invoice for £162.50. Due to circumstances beyond my control this account has not yet been settled, but I am pleased to inform you that if you re-submit the account next month, your request will receive sympathetic consideration.

Yours, etc.

COMPUTER, blaming the   Even if your firm doesn't have a computer, you could be forgiven for inventing the existence of one to carry the can for all your blunders.

I merely make this plea on behalf of all long-suffering customers: if you make the cause of these non-existent computer errors *interesting*, you may even be believed.

For instance, if a customer has placed an order five times and still not received the goods, it just isn't good enough to blame the computer. That's simply a silicon-chip-age version of 'the van's broken down'. Give the thing some personality: 'I'm afraid our computer has taken against customers whose name begins with a W or whose first name is Christopher. It accepts the order then destroys the ledger entry and erases your name from its memory. It does it every time. It's a very personal fault and our engineers are doing all they can to find out why it has taken exception to you and all our other Ws. Can you think of anything you might have done to upset it?'

The first case of 'computer murder' was reported in America recently. A frustrated customer burst into a firm's computer room and pumped six .38 slugs into the blinking, whirring machine, causing massive brain damage and instant technological death.

The attack gave me ideas and it should give you some, too. 'Unfortunately, someone shot the computer' is a pretty damned good excuse for just about anything.

A friend swears that when he phoned his bank in the country to complain about a wrong entry on his statement, a cashier told him, 'Yes, that would have been about the time Smokey had her kittens.'

'Who is Smokey and what the hell have her kittens got to do with my account being wrongly debited?' he inquired.

'Smokey is the bank's cat. Somehow she squeezed under the computer and had her litter there. We had to shut down the computer for two hours while we retrieved the kittens and I'm afraid that one or two errors did occur as a result.'

DANCE, **not wanting to**   When I was a very impressionable age, I approached a Geordie lass who was sitting out a dance at the Rex in Whitley Bay, and asked her if I could have the honour of the next one. 'Ee,' she said, 'dance with my friend, I'm sweatin'.'

This story illustrates not one but *two* successful solutions to the problem of turning down a request to dance without hurting the other person's feelings: (a) find an overpoweringly unpleasant physical reason that will ensure the other person won't want to dance with you and (b) sub-contract the invitation to a friend. (An alternative to (a) would be to accept the invitation to dance but to make it conditional: 'Can you give me five minutes – my artificial limb became unhitched halfway through the eightsome reel.')

On the other hand, you may prefer to adopt the more simple tactic used with great success over the years by Warren Beatty, the well-known ladies' man who makes and appears in films. When asked to dance, he replies, 'Thank you, but I *don't* dance.' Not 'I can't dance', note. Not 'I won't dance.' But 'I *don't* dance.' There is an utter finality about the way Beatty says it that discourages any further discussion of the subject by the forward females who fancy a fox-trot.

DELIVERY, non- Someone, somewhere is expecting from you something which is never going to arrive. Why? Because you never sent it, that's why. They must never know this.

The perfect excuse of 1912 went something like this: 'I really can't understand why you haven't received it yet. I myself took it to the White Star line's freight depot and was assured that it was being sent express cargo on the *SS Titanic*.'

Seventy years later, newsworthy events still provide watertight alibis. Perhaps you gave it to a friend to post who said: 'I'll pop it in the box on my way back from the Iranian embassy.' Or maybe an over-vigilant Post Office worker didn't like the look of the package and immersed it in a bucket of water until the Bomb Squad could put sandbags round it and detonate it. Every day the newspapers report fires, explosions, and crashes which could account for the loss of any number of things you have never sent off.

Statistically the odds are heavily against a letter or parcel being 'lost in the post' and even more loaded against you being believed if anything really did disappear in this way.

However, it's amazing how often wrongly addressed letters never reach their destinations, as is demonstrated by the following conversation:

'You should have had it by now. It went off, let me see now, must have been a week ago.'

'Well I never received it.'

'Let me check your address. Number 23 Eslington Terrace . . .'

'No! It's Number *33*.'

'Well then, that explains everything.'

Another possibility is that, as a precaution against loss, you marked your own name and address on the back so distinctly that a sorter mistook the sender for the addressee and delivered it back to you . . . the day after you left home for three weeks' holiday.

Failure to meet promised delivery dates

The usual reasons advanced by our imaginative captains of industry are: Christmas, staff shortages, a strike at the component factory, a fire at the works, a hold-up at the docks, the annual holidays, the Russian invasion of Afghanistan, and sickness.

The latest, recorded by Keith Waterhouse in the *Daily Mirror*, goes like this: 'We regret the delay in expediting your esteemed order. Due to redundancies in our packing department we are at present short of staff.'

An excuse more likely to win sympathy from the put-upon customer would go something like this:

'Our sales manager Ron Osborne has been kidnapped by left-wing guerillas in the Argentine. From what you have told me, your order must have been in Ron's order book at the time he was captured. Negotiations with the guerillas are at a very delicate stage, but we hope to have Ron – and his order book – out by Christmas.

'In the meantime, if we could have a deposit from you, it would help us meet the kidnappers' financial expectations. It means such a lot, this, to poor Ron's wife and three children.'

DOORSTEP SALESMEN The doorstep salesman has a built-in immunity to excuses. He *has* to have: his livelihood depends on it. He is the man (or she is the woman) with a thousand answers.

There is a way, however, of making the door-to-door sales person abandon the pitch even before they have begun. It goes something like this:

'For your own sake, I'll make this as brief as possible. We have two cases of Legionnaire's Disease in this house and I shouldn't even have opened the door to tell you this without a mask on. I won't put you at risk any longer, except to say that if you are sick or feel giddy during the next fourteen days, go and see your doctor immediately.

DRINK, **having to have one** Just as some people are slow to dip their hand into their pocket, so those same people give a very good impersonation of a host who has given up the search for the lost key to the cocktail cabinet.

Life is too short to sit there all night staring into a teacup while dropping hints about the attractive cut-glass tumblers on the sideboard and striking up conversations about the merciful failure of some products, such as whisky, to keep pace with the general rise of the cost-of-living index.

What you need is a *reason* to have a drink, so that you can ask for one the moment it becomes clear you are not going to be offered one. Your reason is our old friend 'a rare medical condition'.

Since birth, you have suffered from a constriction of the capillaries, and a succession of doctors and consultants has treated the disorder with a variety of drugs, the latest of which was costing the Health Service £15 per day.

Recently you have been co-operating in research into the condition, conducted by the capillary constriction unit at Bart's where doctors believe that they have at last discovered a cure: alcohol. They have found that whisky, or an equivalent dose of gin or vodka, taken every four hours, is sufficient to prevent you from blacking out, which is an unhappy consequence of this affliction. *Your next dose is already ten minutes overdue.*

Depending on how well this goes down with your inhospitable host or hostess, you could ask for your next dose 'in advance', pointing out that in four hours' time the pubs will be shut. You ask this only because you find it so sordid, in a public place, to have to remove from your trouser pocket a miniature bottle of spirits and drink the contents.

As you empty the contents of your second glass down your throat, you should condemn the Government bitterly for being so short-sighted and narrow-minded as to refuse to consider your personal request to make this daily 'medicine' available 'on the Health'.

If you don't feel up to spinning a yarn, you might try this: 'You look far too tired to go to all that trouble to make a cup of tea. Let's just settle for some gin.'

DRUNK, being   The point is, you *weren't* drunk. What you were was exceptionally tired due to a combination of too much work (a coach crash during last summer's works outing decimated the department) and too little sleep (you are being woken four or even seven times a night by your sick children/ electrification of the railway line at the bottom of your garden/the necessity to get up to re-anchor the flapping plastic sheet that is acting as your roof while the builders re-timber the top floor).

As if this isn't enough to make anyone slur their words and appear to be unsteady on their feet, you suffer from this rare medical condition which you share with Reggie Bosanquet, a speech impediment which has afflicted you since childhood.

The problem, however, is not yours but Society's. What a sad reflection it is on our times that just because you happen to have a drink in your hand when you cannot enunciate your words and may even

be swaying slightly, *everyone* assumes you must be drunk.

The best excuse ever for being drunk, by the way, came from a man lying in the gutter on Christmas Eve. He told a policeman: 'I'm not drunk. I'm a plumber from the Water Board, this lady's pipe has burst, and I've got my arm through the grate in the pavement to try to free her stop-cock.'

EXTRA TIME, winning   There are times when even the most quick-witted of us need extra time in which to prepare our defence. Here are some well-known phrases or sayings that will buy you those precious seconds, weeks, or years:

I have a complete answer to all the charges made against me, which I will give at the appropriate place and at the appropriate time. Until then, I will not dignify these outrageous allegations with a reply.

I don't have my diary with me at the moment.

Can I come back to you on this one?

Not at the moment.

I am making no plans of any sort at present.

I like the sound of it. Perhaps when I'm feeling better . . .

When can I let you know?

Until I am in possession of all the facts, I would rather not comment.

This is something I will be acting on immediately; the moment I get back from holiday, in fact.

My initial reaction is a favourable one, but I'd like to sleep on it. I'll be in touch in a fortnight's time.

Let me unarrange a few things first.

I can't give you an answer until I receive an all-important piece of information on which everything depends at the moment.

I've made myself a promise not to commit myself to

anything else until I have met all my present obligations. But, certainly, after that . . .

I would like to, but not until I've extricated myself from something I'm very heavily involved in.

Don't go away.

FACE, forgetting someone's (*See also* **Name**, forgetting someone's) Forgetting the face of someone you know or have met even briefly isn't necessarily an indication that you have found them instantly and enduringly forgettable, but that's the way the forgotten face sees it. If *they* can remember *your* face, they reason, why can't *you* remember *theirs?*

You must tell them why. You suffer from 'face-blindness', a little-known condition, similar to dyslexia, which affects the sufferer's visual recognition of faces (and, in some cases, landscapes too, you should add for good measure).

When normal ('face-sighted') people look at a face, they see all the various distinguishing features in the correct place, and their brain automatically stores the 'picture' for future reference. A 'face-blind' person, however, sees a nose, a mouth, two ears, and two eyes unrelated and out of context to each other, and the eye sends no signals to the brain about the composite picture, for reasons no doctor or psychologist has yet been able to discover.

By this time, you will have won your audience's interest, sympathy, and forgiveness. But you must press on lest they should suspect or discover that there is no such affliction. Describe how you once cut your own wife dead at a dinner party in your own home because you failed to recognise her and how you went to the park with your two children and returned home with someone else's.

You must now give a dramatic demonstration of

your handicap. Make an excuse to absent yourself briefly from the company of the person whose face you have just forgotten, and fail to recognise them ten minutes later when you return.

FAILURE: in sport/business/politics I have endeavoured to discover the best of the many excuses put forward for the sinking of the *Titanic* – whether by the shipbuilder who designed the 'unsinkable' liner, the captain who steered her into an iceberg, or the shipping company who assembled this disastrous team of losers.

The winner, by about 5,000 fathoms, is: '*The sea was too calm.*' This was the line taken by one of the look-outs on the night of the tragedy, echoed by Captain Smith before he went down with his ship, and subsequently used by the White Star Line in the official inquiries. They blamed the weather – for being just too fine.

The audacity of the excuse matches the magnitude of the catastrophe. The brilliance of it is that it is *true*. If the sea had been even slightly choppy instead of 'like a millpond' then the iceberg almost certainly would have been sighted in time and 1,522 lives saved. The reason: however invisible a 'berg might be in the North Atlantic, you can always spot it by the waves breaking around its base. But that night there were no waves . . .

Public failure – whether in politics, sport, business, or any field of human endeavour – demands that the blame should be swiftly apportioned on someone or something else. Time after time, the weather carries the can, as it did with the *Titanic*, and still does with British Rail and the Gas and Electricity boards who recoil in shocked surprise that it should snow in January, catching them totally unawares.

The weather is so popular an excuse that property speculator William Stern managed to blame it – metaphorically – for the financial collapse of his business empire. Asked why his companies had gone bankrupt to the tune of £104,390,248, Stern replied: '*The summer was so beautiful that no one could believe it would be replaced by a hard Siberian winter.*' In less poetic moments, Stern blamed the Bank of England 'for keeping the property crash secret'.

Jim Slater, on the other hand, was let down not by the weather but by a monster: '*I created a monster that was beyond my personal control.*' Later, in his book *Return to Go*, the monster assumed a more human form: '*Some of the executives were not of the right moral fibre or ability and, when the markets turned, their limitations became only too obvious.*'

In other words, no one could possibly have foreseen their limitations *before* the collapse of Slater Walker Securities. This is a fine example of what *Management Today* magazine has described as 'management by excuse'.

Bernie Cornfield made the collapse of his £940 million Investors Overseas Service sound like a game of chess that he had played with himself, beating himself through sheer brilliance and skill: '*My problem was that I always have to create problems for myself to solve,*' he said. Later, when charged with fraud, criminal mismanagement, and abetting speculation, he said: '*I am a born leader but not terribly well organised.*'

Most businessmen find it more convenient to blame their failures on strikes, Government policies, inflation, or currency fluctuations. Rolls-Royce chairman Sir Frank McFadzean managed to blame all four in his 1980 annual report announcing losses of £58 million against profits of £11 million the previous year.

Politicians either blame the voters (Ted Heath: '*I told them but they didn't listen*') or the Establishment (John Stonehouse: '*They closed ranks*'). Or they refuse to admit defeat, the excuse here being that they in fact won. Harold Stassen, America's least successful politician, who stood for office for more than twenty years without being elected, always talked about 'my winning life'. He said: '*Superficially, a political defeat appears to be a disaster. But often it is the only means of communicating something you believe in, of seeing your ideals catch fire.*'

Actors blame 'insufficient rehearsal' because that's down to the producer or director; but sportsmen mostly blame the other player for having an unfair advantage.

'*I don't know what he was playing, but it wasn't tennis,*' said Ilie Nastase after his defeat by Borg at Wimbledon in 1980. This is a variation of the well-known boxing excuse, 'He wasn't human', in which the fighter blames his manager for sending him into the ring with a bear or a gorilla.

Muhammad Ali, after his defeat by Joe Frazier in 1971, made it sound as if everything had gone according to plan. '*It's a good feeling to lose,*' he said. Motor-cycle stuntman Evel Knievel just said: 'I gave it my best', after his Snake River jump flopped. But It let him down.

Dave Smith, captain of Berwick Rangers, blamed the fans for his team's 9–0 defeat in the first game of the season. Or rather the *absence* of fans. '*In the past I have felt we deserved better support at our matches,*' he complained in the local paper.

Tradesmen blame the customer: you obviously have the wrong sort of hair, or your feet are too hot. An excuse gaining in popularity by the hour is: 'No one ever complained before.'

Soldiers don't make excuses, because they never

concede defeat, preferring to gloss over their less glorious moments. After Japan had been A-bombed into submission in 1945, Japan's imperial transcript announcing the surrender simply said: '*The war situation has developed, not necessarily to Japan's advantage.*' The author no doubt then went out and disembowelled himself in front of what remained of the Emperor's palace.

FOOD, not finishing hostess's   All of us know that feeling of rising panic at a dinner party when our host or hostess places before us some gastronomic creation of which they are inordinately proud but which has the immediate effect of making one want to rush upstairs and lock the bathroom door.

To leave your plate untouched is tantamount to saying, 'I think this dish stinks'; to eat it is to invite an

even more ungracious demonstration of your disapproval, possibly all over the dinner table; to knock it on the floor is to risk an even larger replacement helping being placed before you.

Thank heavens for allergies which, perversely, compel people to forgo even the foods they love best. Take a deep breath and shovel in one mouthful of the disgusting dish and exclaim, 'This is absolutely *delicious*! What is it?'

As your host or hostess is reeling off the ingredients ('chopped peppers with double cream, cheese sauce, grated almonds, minced veal, avocado with prawns . . .') halt them in mid-sentence and, in the wounded tone of someone who has just discovered they have been cheated out of a pools win, declare, 'Chopped almonds? Oh, no, I just dare not risk it. If I get within five yards of an almond I am covered head to foot by terrible blotches and weals. It's a most embarrassing and uncomfortable allergy.'

To cover yourself, just in case you have eaten almonds on several previous visits to your hosts without suffering the ill-effects you have so graphically described, you should add: 'The extraordinary thing is, I could eat as many almonds as I liked until six months ago.'

In a doctor's presence, this may not wash. In which case you must fall back on: 'I was forced to eat it as a child and as a result have never been able to face it since.'

FORGETTING   The best excuse of all is often the truthful one: you forgot. You are, after all, only human. But there are times when your failure to remember an invitation, a task, an anniversary, is regarded by others as uncaring, negligent, or even insulting.

You can be blamed for forgetfulness but no one can hold you responsible for the consequences of a medical condition about which most people are mercifully ignorant: amnesia. This is your escape route.

There is no such thing as seven-day amnesia, but no one – except, of course, a doctor – knows that. Seven-day amnesia, you can therefore state confidently, is a protective device which is triggered by a traumatic or emotional experience (take your choice of the death of a parent, a car crash, or the disintegration of a meaningful relationship).

This is nature's way, you continue, of maintaining sanity by erasing from the human mind everything – however irrelevant – that transpired during the period when the crisis occurred. Although normal service was resumed immediately afterwards, there are seven 'lost' days in your life during which, for all you know, you may even have murdered someone.

Alternatively, you could be suffering from 'recurring or intermittent amnesia'. This is a spell of forgetfulness, sometimes lasting no longer than half-an-hour, that you have suffered ever since you fell off a garden wall as a child. You can mention that the previous attack was so long ago that you had almost forgotten you were prone to these 'attacks'.

GET IT UP, inability to   Thanks to the profusion (or should it be *con*fusion) of sex-advice books and sex therapists sounding off all the time about psycho-sexual problems, there is no shame these days in Not Getting It Up. At least, there shouldn't be. But a gentleman still owes it to a lady to come up with a face-saving excuse which will leave both of them in the clear if he can't come up with something else.

For this reason it is probably best for the man to blame his (hopefully) temporary embarrassment on someone who isn't there. 'I'm terribly sorry, but for a moment you reminded me so much of my first wife' ought to be good for a month's impotence, especially if he adds: 'We were very much in love in the beginning.'

A fiancée 'who died in tragic circumstances' is also worth having up your pyjama sleeve since, with luck, the living bedmate will regard it as a challenge to exorcise this particular ghost in the most exciting and inventive way.

'Stage Fright' is a legitimate reason for not giving your finest performance and demonstrates, when you describe it thus, that you have a sense of humour (although, if you keep on having first-night nerves, you risk being taken off after a week).

In the same vein, 'I'm never any good first time', is an excuse that an experienced woman will understand, having probably encountered it before; but it is not calculated to arouse sympathy in virgins or circumspect spinsters who don't wish to be reminded at a moment like this that they are one of a cast of thousands.

Any man who has been bitten on the bare bottom by a hornet can justifiably plead Fear Of Open Spaces if he fails to fulfil his potential in the great outdoors, or even in the back of a car. And in a contest of lust-versus-discomfort in a broom closet, discomfort can win every time without loss of face. ('Darling, be reasonable. How can I make love with my left foot jammed in a bucket and a Hoover handle up my bum?')

Good, old-fashioned guilt will always be given sympathetic consideration by Catholic girls, the great plus being that you don't have to be Catholic to claim to experience it. Since so much sexual activity is furtive or illicit anyway, you probably have every reason to be inhibited by guilt. But, if nothing else, it shows you have a conscience and even gives you an opportunity to express your feelings: 'Why should I feel guilty about something so beautiful, so right, so natural . . .?' The answer, possibly, is because you keep expecting her husband to walk through the bedroom door.

Stress, anxiety, and exhaustion are recognised medical causes of impotence and are therefore probably the only *long-term* excuses that will wash. But even if they are the cause of the hitch, they really shouldn't be used the first time, on account of the fact that no woman in her right mind is going to want to take on a new lover who is anxious, exhausted, and torn apart by stress.

The lover who announces, 'I'm sorry about this, but I'm very anxious and exhausted' invites the reply: 'You're right to be anxious, but so far you haven't done anything to exhaust yourself.'

HELPING, reasons for not Some hosts and hostesses believe in making their guests, as they put it, 'sing for their supper'. I take the view that washing up, gardening, decorating, and other household chores are activities in which I participate only in my own home and even then with the greatest reluctance.

When your hosts regard you as part of a non-volunteer work force, getting yourself off the job sheet can take some doing.

The best escape from helping with the washing up I ever saw was at a supper party at the end of which our hostess announced: 'Let's clear up and then go and have another drink.' One of the women guests turned to the hostess's husband and said: 'I simply wouldn't *dare* interfere in Nancy's kitchen', and promptly absented herself to the drawing-room where she sat in front of the fire with a book.

'I'd offer to help with the washing up but I'm dreadfully clumsy' carries an implied threat that if you are press-ganged into helping, you'll get your revenge by breaking something. The excuse needs to be substantiated, nonetheless: 'I inherited two left feet from my father, I'm afraid', followed by an example of your own clumsiness – at someone else's expense, of course.

The best protection you have against manual labour is a bad back. 'My doctor has warned me that if I so much as lift a spade or push a wheelbarrow, I'll be flat on my back for six months in traction.'

The same bad back, of course, prohibits you from raising your right arms above your head holding a paintbrush. Just tell your friends, 'If I did myself an injury, I know you'd never forgive yourself.'

HOME, not lending your

1   For illicit sex

Many years ago I took a new girl friend home to my
bachelor flat for the first time. As I put my key into the
door, she said: 'Do you mind if we go somewhere else?
I just couldn't – not here.' She then revealed that she
had slept in my bed regularly for a year with a married
colleague of mine who used to borrow my flat.

That was the day I stopped lending out a love nest
to my friends. If my flat was going to hold memories
for pretty girls, I reasoned, I ought to be included in
those memories. This is now *my* excuse for keeping
adulterous male friends out of my bedroom.

'I like your wife/husband too much' is another
perfectly reasonable objection to not wanting to
change your sheets when you come home from work.
Even if you *don't* know the partner who is being
cheated on, the point is you *might* meet them socially
at some time and become friends. When the affair is
discovered and the recriminations are flying, it's
going to be all your fault for providing the opportunity and the Dunlopillo mattress. *You'll* be the one
who wrecked the marriage.

But desperate, sex-starved lovers can be very
persuasive and, by refusing a request on these
grounds, you may find yourself backing down in the
end on humanitarian grounds.

In these circumstances, there is only one way of
putting an end to the debate once and for all. A
married person is already occupying your bed when
you're not. Somebody you both know very well but
whose identity you could not possibly reveal because
it would mean breaking a confidence. They have
bagged your bed first and, judging by the debris they
leave behind, the affair looks like continuing
indefinitely.

2 *To friends and freeloaders*

Many of us, fond as we are of our friends, don't like the idea of them burning a hole in our sitting-room carpet, unearthing, while searching for a duster, the love letters we wrote twenty years ago, or breaking an irreplaceable ornament of great sentimental value. It's unreasonable of us, I know, but unreasonable is what we are.

But if burning holes in sitting-room carpets puts a strain on friendships, so does declining to lend friends your home when you're away. After all, they argue, you're not using the place. What kind of people do you imagine they are?

The answer must be that they are the kind of people to whom you would love to lend your home if it weren't impossible, for one of the following reasons: While you are away . . .

The place is being redecorated/rewired.

The rodent officer is laying poisoned bait in every room in an attempt to solve once and for all your vermin problem. It is essential that no human activity should disturb the roaming mice or rats.

Arrangements have already been made for the telephone and electricity to be disconnected during your absence. This is a precaution you always take and at this stage it cannot be reversed.

Your landlords are enforcing to the letter a clause of your lease that prohibits anyone except your next of kin from occupying the flat in your absence. The landlords are just looking for a chance to throw you out, following your success in having the rent halved by the Rent Officer last year.

All the beds, mattresses, and curtains have been removed by an industrial upholstery and dry-cleaning contractor to be resprung or cleaned.

Your 'silent partner' in the flat or house will be staying for a day or two with a lady friend. He's a globe-trotting businessman who pays a substantial percentage of your overheads in return for a pied-à-terre during the few days a year he is in town. This is such a perfect arrangement, you would hate to do anything to upset it.

HOSPITALITY, **failure to return** No one minds if hospitality isn't returned immediately, just so long as there is a promise and some expectation of it in the not-too-distant future. The moment you have sorted out your house or flat, in fact.

The impression to create is that of your home being furnished and decorated in readiness for these your very special guests. You would have them round to dinner tomorrow *but you don't yet have a table*. (The fact that you have been living there for six-and-a-half years is an indication of the painstaking preparations that are being made for The Visit.)

ILLNESS **and** INJURIES Illness has been dramatically devalued as an excuse by over-use and hypochondria. And also, it needs to be said, by people with genuine illnesses and injuries fighting bravely on. Like the actress who died on stage of cancer, and Prince Charles, who attended an official dinner only hours after falling off his polo pony and suffering cuts and concussion. They ruin it for the rest of us who have been telling everyone for years that the reason we couldn't make it was because we had a headache.

As excuses for failure of any sort, illnesses and injuries can be divided starkly into two: the acceptable and the downright unbelievable. The latter should be avoided like, well, the plague:

ACCEPTABLE	UNBELIEVABLE
Hepatitis	'Flu
Mumps (in men)	Migraine
Suspected heart attack	Gastric 'flu
Having a baby (day before labour only)	Sprained ankle
	Slipped disc
Any terminal disease	'Up all night'
Haemorrhaging from a coil	'Been sick'
	Period pains
Vasectomy stitches broken	Running a temperature
Root canal therapy	'Some sort of stomach bug'
Wasp sting inside mouth	
Viral pneumonia	Tennis elbow
Any organ 'on the blink'	Broken limb

INDUSTRIAL DISPUTES, usefulness of

Industrial disputes are an accepted disruption of our everyday lives. They immobilise us, delay us, frustrate our very best intentions. Where would we be without them?

As excuses, they are a veritable goldmine. Used imaginatively, they provide a good reason for not doing just about anything we don't want to do and for not having done just about everything we ought to have done. But their credibility rating depends not so much on the headline space that a particular dispute attracts but on your skilful manipulation of the likely effects of that dispute.

For instance, 'We won't be able to come and see you on Sunday after all, because of the petrol-tanker drivers' dispute' is too convenient, too easy, too wet a get-out. It leaves the other people thinking (rightly), 'They could have got here if they had really wanted to' and they will resent your lack of imagination in looking no further than the front page of your newspaper for a reason not to visit them.

The secret is to use as your excuse a *knock-on effect*

of the tanker drivers' dispute. Thus: 'We're fortunate enough to have plenty of petrol – more than enough to visit you five times – but because of the tanker drivers' dispute Harry's firm are sending him to Manchester a day early in case the situation in the North-West worsens next week. Isn't it infuriating?'

Similarly, a rail strike is not a good enough reason for not turning up for work. But the same rail strike could make it necessary for you to drive your crippled mother twenty-two miles to an important hospital appointment, wait, then bring her home again.

Creative excusers will not be satisfied to hide behind the headline-grabbing dispute. They will scan the inside pages of the *Daily Telegraph*, looking for minor industrial squabbles that, with a little dressing up, could have far-reaching implications and effects on their own private and professional lives. Within twenty-four hours of a work-to-rule by German steelworkers in Solingen, for example, they will have created a shortage of cider casks in Taunton.

The great value of industrial disputes as excuses is that, even when the country *isn't* being paralysed by two hundred different disputes, the threat is an ever-present one. Your ultimate strike excuse for being unable to do something is, therefore, that you were too busy panic-buying.

INVITE, forgetting to   Whenever more than two people are gathered together in one place, someone's nose is going to be put out of joint. Someone who thinks he or she ought to be there, but isn't, because (a) you didn't want them to be there or (b) you intended them to be present but forgot to invite them. Whether the injured party is an aunt who wasn't invited to the wedding, or a colleague at work who was excluded from a meeting, you will have some explaining to do.

There are a number of possibilities open to you.

1   An innocent mistake has occurred which is deeply regretted.

A thought B had issued the invitation and B was firmly under the impression that A had. Consequently, neither did. C wrongly assumed that either A or B would, so did nothing, either.

A variation of this excuse is that the absent guest *was* invited, in so far as their name appeared on the first and second drafts of the invitation list. The list was subsequently given to a secretary, or some other outsider, to type out and at this stage the name was accidentally left off. The possibility of a typing error didn't occur to you, so no double-check was made and the omission went unnoticed.

Another possibility is that, to ensure that everyone you wanted to be there was invited, you painstakingly drew up the invitation list from your address book. Unfortunately, a page was missing from the book and you just never noticed. As a result, the Kanes, the Keenans, the Kennedys, and the Kings aren't talking to you either. Admittedly, the Kinghorns *were* there, but only because, for some inexplicable reason, they were entered in your book under 'R'.

2   No invitation was issued because no one was invited.

The gathering was impromptu and unplanned, occasioned by the coincidence of four or five people being in the same place at the same time, all for different reasons.

3   The occasion wasn't 'the real thing'.

It was merely a dress rehearsal for the Great Event to which they *will* of course be invited when a date is fixed.

4   Because of the number of people involved, or the lack of space, you decided to have two 'sittings', distributing the important guests equally over the two events.

But the first, to which they weren't invited because you needed them badly at the second, was such a dismal failure that you have now abandoned plans for the second.

5 *They were 'far too important' to be there.*

No good, this, for a social gaffe, but highly effective at work or public functions. The argument here is, they weren't invited because you needed them to 'hold the fort' in everyone else's absence. The work they are engaged on is far too important to break off for what amounted to little more than chit-chat among colleagues. Besides, the only important things that were discussed you had privately informed them about weeks in advance.

LATE ARRIVAL If there's one thing more irritating than being kept waiting, it's being told by the surprised latecomer, 'the traffic was *terrible*.' I mean, when wasn't the traffic terrible?

On the other hand, anyone can be forgiven for being late if something totally unforeseen happens to them as they hurry to their appointment. Here are just some of the things that could prevent you from arriving on time without the delay reflecting on you badly in any way.

1 You were mistaken for Lord Lucan and detained by the police. The fact that you bear no resemblance to the vanished Earl, or that you are a woman, need not throw doubt on the veracity of your story. On the contrary. The last person Lord Lucan is going to look like if he is still alive is Lord Lucan.

2 You thought you were in Durban. Or, to be more precise, your digital quartz 24-hour international time-zoned watch thought you were in Durban and was showing a read-out of Durban time instead of GMT. This malfunction led you to believe

that you had two hours more time than you in fact did. At moments like this, you remark, you wonder whether we wouldn't all be better off going back to sundials.

3   A jobless teenager threw himself in front of your tube train. This is a more melodramatic, more topical version of, 'I'm sorry I'm late – I had to wait more than forty minutes for a No. 52' – an event so predictable, an excuse so boring, that the person you have kept waiting will wish you had thrown yourself under the said No. 52. On the other hand, no one could have foreseen that an unemployed youngster would choose your tube train to convey himself to the great Job Centre in the sky.

4   The Prime Minister kept you waiting. Just as you are about to be denounced as a liar, as well as a loiterer, you explain that you have come from 10 Downing Street where you have been presenting a petition to Mrs T demanding a ban of nuclear-waste test-boring in the Cheviots.

5   A horse rolled on you. This explanation will so baffle people that they will hesitate to make further inquiries into the nature of the accident.

6   You were stuck in a lift – with, it needs to be said, an Ethiopian mural painter, and a member of the SAS who lowered himself through a trap door in the lift floor and abseiled to freedom down the shaft two hours before you and the Ethiopian mural artist could be rescued by the fire brigade.

7   The cloakroom attendant at the restaurant where you had lunch yesterday inadvertently gave you someone else's coat, identical in every respect to your own. You were returning it and collecting in return your own coat, which had your wallet containing £62 in the left-hand pocket.

8   You were given someone else's *car* by mistake when you went to collect your own from the garage.

The mix-up came to light when its rightful owner reported it missing – and an alert patrol-car officer arrested you and impounded the 'stolen' vehicle you had the misfortune to believe was your own.

9   You found a goshawk with a broken wing and had to take it to an RSPCA sanctuary.

LEAVING EARLY

From a social engagement

It is 10.30 pm and the friends who are entertaining you are not being very entertaining. Suddenly you wish you were at home in bed. But to leave so soon after dinner would be less than polite. Unless . . .

'Dammit!' you exclaim, looking at your watch. 'I forgot to set the video recorder to tape *Some Like It Hot* at 11.15.'

'Watch it here,' says your obliging host. 'I don't mind seeing it again. It's a wonderfully funny film.'

'Thank you, but I've seen it half a dozen times,' you reply. 'No, I promised to record it for a friend who's abroad. I can't let him down because he's always taping programmes for me when I'm away.'

'You can record it on ours,' says your too obliging host. 'Your video is a VHS like ours, isn't it?'

'Yes,' you say, 'but our friend left *his* video with us when he went away and unfortunately it's a Betamax. The tape wouldn't be compatible.'

You thank your hosts profusely for their hospitality and head home for an early night.

Having to drive the baby-sitter home is a fairly good exit line, too, but not before 11 pm. If you want to leave any earlier than that, your baby-sitter has to be in the middle of her 'O' levels or sitting the finals of her SRN exams, with a crucial practical at 8.30 the following morning ('It just wouldn't be fair . . .').

Calling your baby-sitter to make sure everything's all right – and getting no reply – is a good enough excuse to leave five minutes after you arrived, especially if you suddenly remember you left an unguarded four-bar electric fire in your bedroom ('I couldn't relax or enjoy myself, not knowing . . .'). Dial a number you know will never answer, like a police station, a national newspaper, or one of the Post Office information services.

An epileptic, diabetic, and alcoholic next-door neighbour whom you have taken under your wing is good for a quick getaway, too. Tell everyone about her latest binge and voice your fears about finding her in a coma after it's too late to do anything. ('I'd never forgive myself if I didn't look in.')

Friends arriving from abroad are insufficient reason to leave a pleasant social occasion early, because you should have either brought them with you or made arrangements in your absence for them to gain entry to your home and await your return. The solution here is to have done just that – to have left the keys under a loose brick – but forgotten to warn your visitors about switching off the burglar alarm.

The expectation of a telephone call from abroad doesn't cut much ice these days and 'I've got to be up early' is merely an admission of a lack of stamina on your part. 'My doctor says I must be in bed by 11 pm every night for six months' is OK, provided that you indicate the medical grounds and make the excuse in advance as a condition of your acceptance of the invitation.

From work

Since you are presumably being paid for the early cut, your excuse should be of a worthy or medical nature. 'I have to give blood' passes on both these counts.

'I've got an appointment at the Family Planning

clinic' is something you could and should have arranged in your own time, since it is directly related to recreation, but 'I don't wish to avail myself of the company's generous maternity leave and benefits, so would it be all right if I kept a 2 pm appointment at the clinic to have a coil fitted?' almost qualifies you for an award to industry.

'I have to have my dressing changed' sounds unpleasant and sinister enough to deter all but the strictest disciplinarian from inquiring further about the nature of the sore or injury. But should such questions be asked, the mention of an abscess, without specifying on which part of your body it is to be found, should terminate the conversation and win you the permission you seek. You may even be told to take tomorrow off.

A visit at home from two police officers investigating a robbery you *almost* witnessed ('they said they didn't want to embarrass me by interviewing me at work') will also strike an authentic note, especially when you report next day that the questions they asked seemed to you to be wholly irrelevant.

Interesting reasons to leave work early are guaranteed to attract more sympathy than boring, stereotyped requests. For instance, if your aunt hid a large sum of money and jewels before she died, what would be more natural for you than to ask a medium to arrange a seance to contact your aunt to inquire about its whereabouts?

LETTERS, failure to answer

Dear Anne and Harry,

I am sorry, too, that you never received a reply to your letter of August 22nd, as I would have loved to come. The truth of the matter is, your letter containing the invitation reached me only at the weekend, via the local vicar. When he called on me with it, I was as puzzled as you no doubt are now, so let me explain.

Your letter was one of three addressed to me that were found in a wellington boot bought at the church's summer fête. Obviously the boot was one of the pair that I gave to the jumble sale; but how did the letters – unopened – come to be in the boot?

This can only be speculation, of course, but it can be the only explanation. Around the time you wrote to me, Fanny and I shifted some furniture in the hall. As you know, having visited our home many times, a row of wellington boots always stands to the left of the front door. Both of us remember temporarily moving these boots out of our way to give ourselves more elbow room, and for more than half-an-hour, I suppose, the boots stood *under* the front door. If the postman put any letters through the letter-box during this time they would have dropped straight into a boot, it now occurs to us in retrospect. When, a fortnight later, we parcelled up some old clothes etc. for the jumble, the last thing we thought of doing was checking the wellies for mail.

I can understand you being upset, but a telephone call at the time would have confirmed that we never received your letter. And, as I hope you now realise, there sometimes *is* a perfectly good excuse for a wholly innocent discourtesy.

Yours ever,

Dear Sir,

When I received this morning your curt reminder of the conditions laid down by you in agreeing to my overdraft, I realised that I had never seen the said conditions. This wouldn't be the first letter to go missing recently, so I at once (for reasons which will become apparent) telephoned the estate agents handling the sale of the empty house next door.

One of their representatives very kindly called round with the keys to the house and there, as I suspected, was your letter along with half-a-dozen others addressed to me but put by the postman through the wrong front door. I have taken up the matter with the Post Office.

In the meantime, I will of course give you the undertakings you seek; but not having received your letter until today, I have not had the benefit of your guidelines for the past month. I would therefore be grateful if you would honour any cheques dated prior to today.

Yours faithfully,

Dear Aunt Susan,

I feel a real heel for not coming to see you in hospital, and so does Fanny, but we only got your card today. No, not the Post Office's fault for a change! Your card has been glued to the bottom of a tea tray for the past six weeks and would still be there if it wasn't for our new daily who has a fixation about cleaning *underneath* everything.

I can only think that on the bottom of the tray there must have been some of that very delicious (but very sticky) heather honey you so kindly gave us for Christmas and that the tray was placed on top of the mail on the dining-room table at breakfast before I had a chance to read it. From now on, Superglue is out! I'm sticking (so to speak) to your heather honey.

Hoping you're now well on the road to recovery, despite the lack of bedside visitors.

Fondest best wishes from us both,

Dear Mr Edwards,

Just as I thought! I *did* in fact write to you in May, cancelling the order. What I omitted to do, however, was to post the letter. I placed the envelope in the left-hand jacket pocket of my lightweight linen suit, intending to pop it into a letterbox on the way to work, but for some reason I forgot. Because of the cold, wet, and windy summer we've had, that was the last time I have worn the suit – until the warm spell we've been enjoying this week, when I discovered the letter.

I hope this clears up what might have been an unfortunate misunderstanding.

Yours sincerely,

L **IE, being caught telling a** If you're unfortunate enough to be caught telling a lie, the chances of lying your way out of your predicament successfully are very slender indeed, because anything you say now is going to be subject to close scrutiny and regarded with grave suspicion. Put out of your mind, therefore, any thought of attempting to pass off your lie as 'an honest mistake'.

Your best bet is to present yourself as an honest man forced by circumstances into the distasteful position of *having* to tell an untruth. You did this not to further your own interests, but to protect others, as will become clear shortly. More than this you cannot say at the moment, because by being caught telling this untruth you have already let down quite enough those you sought to protect.

An equally honourable motive for lying is that you did it to protect the person to whom you told this untruth. Such is your esteem and affection for them you could not bear to hurt or disappoint them by confronting them with the unpalatable truth. It was your intention, after telling this lie, vigorously to set about changing the various relevant circumstances so that in six months' time you could hold your head up and repeat this 'lie' and be telling the truth. The 'lie' was therefore no more than a stop-gap measure. The *next* half-year profit figures *will* be as good as you pretended the last half-year figures were.

When a past lie catches up with you, the best solution is to plead insanity, while making it clear that you have now fully recovered your faculties. You lied because, in your distressed and emotional state at that time, you were incapable of distinguishing between the truth and what you wanted the truth to be. This is what your psychiatrist has since told you, and he has no reason to lie.

LOVE, declining to make (*See also* **Pass**, turning down a) Turning down a loved one, or even an unloved one, without detonating a row or a fit of the sulks, is like defusing a sophisticated time-bomb booby-trapped with anti-handling devices. The secret – your only hope of success, in fact – is to convince your partner that there is nothing personal in it.

'I fancy *you* like mad, but not *it*', is a face-saving formula which will grant you a reprieve in any 'regularised' relationship. It's not you, it's not them, it's It. The same It that has made it rain all summer, turned monsoons into a drought, and caused polar bears to attempt to swim towards Africa. What's going on? You wish you knew, but personally you blame the Russians.

A fanciful variation is, 'I fancy *you* like mad, but not *now*.' In other words, go for an adjournment in the hope that, when the appointed hour arrives, your partner's libido will have gone into a decline or your own will have been restored. Why don't you fancy it now? It's your biorhythms. Your body clock's all wrong and according to your 'chart' the best time is going to be tomorrow morning/tonight/lunchtime/next week. You know jolly well that if you give in to your persistent partner now, you can't be certain of getting it from them then, when you will be at your mental, emotional, and physical peak.

Your body clock – it needs to be established for the future safety of this excuse – is subject to change, your biorhythmic peaks switching from morning to night and back again at short notice.

NOT ANOTHER HEADACHE?

The words 'We have a contraceptive problem' not only involve your partner in your excuse but will also quite likely put him or her off the whole idea of sex, bearing in mind the possible outcome. Easier for a woman than a man, this, since more women than men now shoulder the burden of responsibility for contraception. The possibilities are almost endless:

You suspect your coil has fallen out.
You think it may have become dislodged.
You stopped taking the Pill nine days ago because it was making you feel nauseous. Would it be wise to take a chance?

You're fresh out of contraceptive foam/pessaries.
You found the cat playing with your Dutch cap under the bed. You don't think he perforated it, but with those needle-sharp claws . . .

Men don't have so many options for abstinence on contraceptive grounds. Either you inadvertently sent the last packet of condoms to the laundry in the pocket of your pyjama jacket, or 'some strange things' have been happening recently that lead you to believe that your vasectomy may have reversed itself.

You can hardly spring previously unknown medical grounds on a spouse or intimate acquaintance, so it has to be a pain-versus-pleasure contest, in which pain will, you fear, come out on top.

Pains for her: menstruation, ovulation, or any other potentially agonising gynaecological problem, including coil-induced cramps, cystitis, thrush, or other mysterious below-the belt aches.

Pains for him: a visitation of thrush which stings but isn't necessarily occasioned by sexual misconduct (though it *is* infectious) or, indeed, any other tenderness around his Tenderest Parts, such as boils, mystery inflammations, etc.

For him or her: a self-dislocating hip which needs a night's rest to put itself back into place.

I mention in passing that, at the time of writing, the very latest trend sweeping America is celibacy. *Not* making love apparently is all the rage and it has even caught on with married couples, who claim that abstinence allows them to be 'more spiritual' together. An announcement therefore that you would like to give celibacy a try might just work if your partner is very trend-conscious. But if I were you, don't plan to persevere with it. You might end up being celibate for rather longer than you planned.

MONEY, not lending   Either you have got it and don't want to part with it, or you haven't got it, in which case you can't lend it even if you wanted to. Either way, the answer is No. They shouldn't have asked, but the onus is now on you to take steps to ensure that your refusal doesn't offend.

'I always make it a rule never to lend money to friends', has a firmness, a fairness, and a finality that you can temper by adding: 'I value our friendship far too much to put you under any sort of financial obligation to me. This was the very first lesson I learned from my father and, if you think about it, you will realise how right he was.' With luck, the matter will never be raised again.

Another way of saying No is to counter the request by holding out the begging bowl yourself: 'What an extraordinary coincidence. *I* was just about to ask *YOU* for a loan, but I had a much larger sum in mind, I'm ashamed to admit. Obviously we're in the same dire financial straits. God, isn't it awful being broke? Look, if you do find someone who will lend it to you, ask them for a bit more than you need and you might then be able to help *me* out . . .'

The answer, 'I'd lend it to you if I had it' for any sum under £500 is simply not believable even if it's true. They wouldn't have asked you if they weren't fairly certain you had it.

NAME, forgetting someone's   (*See also* **Face**, forgetting someone's)   Just as 'face blindness' causes the unfortunate victim to forget faces, so 'name deafness' renders others incapable of remembering names.

Name-deaf people, like dyslexia sufferers, are otherwise normal and often enjoy above-average intelligence; but for reasons still largely unknown, their brains are unable to assimilate names. This condition is known as Dyslexanoma.

When someone says to you 'Hello, I'm Fred Brown', your ears receive the message but fail to transmit all of it to the brain, which records only the words, 'Hello, I'm . . .'

The handicap is a major social embarrassment, of course, not only because you can rarely recall the names of even close friends and associates: for many years you have had to have name tapes sewn on to the cuffs of all your shirts so that you could introduce *yourself* to people. In fact, before the banks started printing customers' names on individual cheques, you had a chequebook with your name specially imprinted, so that you knew what name to sign on the bottom line.

If the person whose name you have forgotten is a doctor or a psychologist, of course, you obviously can't shoot them this line. Your excuse should be that on the day you met, you underwent hypnosis to try to stop you smoking. An unfortunate side effect was that the treatment erased from your mind everything else that transpired that day.

OVERDRAWN, reasons for being   It is quite possible that the reason you are £642.87 overdrawn at the bank is that your crippled grandmother, who has come to live with you, is putting an ever-increasing strain on your household budget with her dissolute sherry-drinking habits.

Unfortunately, your bank manager runs a bank, not a registered charity, and he will be quick to point this out if you tell him the truth. The cause of your temporary embarrassment therefore has to be something that he understands. Something of a technical rather than a human nature, eliminating flesh and blood, greed or need, generosity or compassion.

You are the victim of a silicon-chip malfunction. What has happened is this:

To make sure you stayed in credit, you have been conscientiously calculating, then noting, the new balance of your account every time you write a cheque or pay in money. But, unknown to you, the pocket calculator that has been assisting you in this responsible chore developed a fault on the plus and minus keys, reversing their respective functions.

Money that you had paid into your account was being deducted in your calculations, and cheques you were writing out were being credited in your cheque-stub notes. This led you erroneously to believe that you were £642.87 in credit, whereas you were in fact £642.87 overdrawn.

Your attitude should be one of deep gratitude that your bank manager has brought this technological fault to light before a serious mistake could occur.

OVERSLEEPING   (*See also* **Work**, being late for)   Oversleeping is an unacceptable excuse for being absent or late unless there is a highly original reason which no one could have foreseen. The following, I humbly suggest, come into this category:

1   You woke up at 6 am with a blinding headache. You fumbled in the drawer of your bedside table for a bottle of Panadol and took three. Only they weren't Panadol, as you discovered to your lasting embarrassment at ten past six that evening when your husband/wife returned home from work and woke you by slapping your face and applying cold flannels to various tender parts of your body. They were Mogadon sleeping tablets.

2   You set the alarm of your new, wafer-thin mini-calculator for 7 am and turned in early. Some time later, your wife followed you to bed and saw on the bedside table what, in the half-light, she immediately recognised as an After Eight chocolate mint. She was horrified, since you are both on strict diets, and removed temptation from your side by flushing the 'choc' down the loo.

PAINTING, hanging upside down   This is a true story. A famous painter is taken proudly by his host and hostess into their drawing-room, where one of his pictures is hanging. 'Doesn't it look marvellous?' they tell the artist, thanking him for sharing his genius with others.

'But you have hung it upside down!' exclaims the artist.

'I know,' says the quick-thinking hostess. 'This is the room my husband and I practise yoga in.'

PARTICIPATING, reasons for not   Whenever people form themselves into a group – whether to play cards, to go for a Sunday afternoon walk or to raise money for some worthy cause – they invariably feel the need to involve someone else in their activities: you.

All *you* want, on the other hand, is to be left alone. You don't *want* to come out to play. They must never know this because the moment they do, they will consider it a personal challenge to get you to join in.

Your escape is that you have a previous engagement – with yourself. Sunday afternoon, you explain regretfully, is the time you set aside every week to dig the garden/write poetry/do the accounts/play with the children/meditate. You *always* have and *always* will. You are, alas, a creature of habit and this weekly appointment with yourself is sacred. You have promised yourself that you will never break it and you cannot permit yourself to let yourself down.

If you don't fancy the idea of casting yourself into the role of creature of habit, then you will probably have to invoke the 'aversion therapy' excuse. Your explanation for declining to take part in the activity being proposed is that you have already done it to death. For them, it is fun; for you, it opens the floodgates of an unpleasant childhood memory.

For instance, 'My mother took me on ten-mile walks every day from the age of three and I've loathed walking ever since' is a perfectly good reason for wanting to watch television instead of being dragged up a hill by your energetic host and hostess.

'I loved poker until I spent four years in the Navy doing nothing else except playing poker' is an equally good reason for never sitting at a card table again.

PASS, turning down a   (*See also* **Love**, declining to make)   These are some of the more convincing arguments that have been advanced by various ladies of my acquaintance over the years for not consummating our relationship. In my defence, I can only say that, at the time, they seemed like very good

reasons for not pressing my case any further, or
indeed for pressing anything else any further.

I like you too much.
I don't like you enough.
I'd like to, but Mecca don't allow it until after the
    Miss World contest.
You can't afford me, sonny.
We might start the dog barking.
We'd only wake up the baby.
I'm under the doctor at the moment.
We're still not far enough from the shore.
My coil dropped out this morning.
My brothers in Sicily wouldn't like it.
My sunburn hurts too much.
We might drown.
Not in the sand.
We'd break the deck chair.
All I want right now is a nice cup of tea.
My husband is due back at any minute.
I think the house is on fire.
We're due into King's Cross in three minutes.
We might get locked into the building.
I've just come off the Pill.
Our star signs are all wrong. It would be a disaster.
Why can't we wait until we're married?
I'm going to forget you ever said that.
The usherette might shine her torch on us.
I'm tired. Why don't you ask my friend?
I feel far too maternal towards you.
But you're just like a brother to me.
The walls are paper thin. I wouldn't enjoy it.
The chandelier in the room below would wake up
    the whole house.
It's the wrong time of the month.
I couldn't, not with the goldfish watching.
Couldn't we play tennis instead?

I made myself a promise two years ago and I intend
   to keep it.
Not so soon after lunch.
Not after church!
May I think about it please?
I never sleep with a man on our first date.
The moment has gone. We left it too long.
I don't want to lose your respect.
If I went to bed with you, I'd fall in love with you,
   and I don't want to do that.
I'd miss my bus.
Can it wait until I've moved my car to another
   meter?
I couldn't, not in my parents' house.
I never play away.
I only play away.
Everyone would see the cable-car rocking.
I'm not that sort of girl.

There was a time when this section could have
ended quite happily here, but as more and more
women take the sexual initiative, it has become
incumbent on us men to find face-saving formulas to
get ourselves out of a corner from time to time. A
'minor but persistent infection' is a powerful
deterrent.

If you can see the situation developing in advance,
the trick is to ask for a glass of water and then make a
performance out of swallowing some pills – for real, if
you have any on you, or pretend, if you haven't. No
woman will be able to resist asking what the tablets
are for, whereupon you reply, with feigned embarrassment, 'Oh, nothing important, just one of those
stubborn little infections.' You then add, 'I shouldn't
really be drinking alcohol, but what the hell', and
change the subject, shifting your buttocks in apparent
discomfort.

If there's no time to take cover, you have to come straight out with it – the excuse, that is. Try to assume the wounded desperation of a starving man who has trodden on his false teeth just as he is being handed a juicy T-bone steak and announce: 'There's nothing I'd like more, frankly, but we have a slight social problem to contend with. Can we have a rain check until my doctor hands me back my permit?'

Married men who don't want to tarnish their reputations may prefer to hide behind hyper-fertility. 'It's only fair to tell you that at the time all my five children were conceived my wife was on the Pill *and* had a coil fitted' could make a nun out of a nymphomaniac.

There is another deterrent which should halt even the most determined man-molester in her tracks, but you may not want to take the risk of it being spread about. It is simply this: 'I'm afraid I'm gay with absolutely *no* bi-sexual tendencies.'

PERSONAL REASONS As excuses go, 'for personal reasons' is about as unforthcoming an explanation as you can get. It reveals nothing, except that the self-excuser considers that he/she is completely excused, for reasons which they do not propose to disclose.

In an age when total strangers will wander up and tell you the most intimate and lurid details about themselves, 'personal reasons' has an intriguing, old-fashioned secrecy about it. What can they be, these personal reasons?

A terminal illness, perhaps? If so, who has it? What is it? An embarrassing sore? If so, on what part of the body? A scandal that has not yet broken? If so, who are the parties involved? What is so shameful or so secret that it cannot be revealed?

The possibilities are boundless and while the imagination is working overtime, one's critical faculties are failing to consider the possibility that these 'personal reasons' are just a game of golf.

For all these reasons, and because people don't like to pry into private grief, it is an invaluable occasional weapon in your armoury of excuses. Used with restraint and discretion, it's good for a day off from work any time, and will get you off the hook with many of the people you have sinned against, providing they don't know you too personally, of course.

Bear in mind that, long after your 'personal reasons' have been accepted as an excuse and forgotten by you, people will still be wondering just what the big secret was all about. You must not disappoint them therefore when they subsequently inquire about your personal problems.

Just tell them: 'Much better, thank you – for the moment.'

POLICE, excuses that wash with Policemen and lawyers call excuses 'mitigating circumstances'. Just how mitigating the circumstances are depends on (a) whether your explanation is believed and (b) whether it strikes a sympathetic chord in the listener.

Prince Philip succeeded on both counts when he was pulled up for speeding on the eve of his wedding. He told the officer: 'I am Prince Philip and I'm on my way to see the Archbishop of Canterbury. I'm a bit late and I didn't want to keep His Grace waiting.' You could try this one yourself, but I can't promise that the patrol-car driver will stand to attention, salute you, and wish you every happiness for the future.

The police, like magistrates and judges, have to be satisfied with your explanation and they are hard men and women to please. A policeman in Somerset apprehended a Polish miner in a local shop in the middle of the night. The officer subsequently gave this evidence against the Pole at Somerset Assizes:

'*I cautioned him and asked him if he had any explanation for his presence in the shop at that time of night. He made a long reply in a language which I subsequently ascertained to be Polish. I told him that I was not satisfied with his explanation and arrested him.*'

. The moral of this story is: if you've got a good excuse, make it in English and not Polish.

Some excuses don't even work in English, of course. Like the youth arrested for riding his motor-cycle on the pavement. Asked what he was doing on the footpath, he replied: 'I can't ride on the road yet because I don't have a licence and haven't passed my test.'

Ignorance of the law is no excuse. In fact it has an aggravating effect on policemen and magistrates. Nor is 'But *everyone* does it' which was the mitigating circumstances pleaded by Charlie Chaplin when he

was accused of a sex offence back in the prim and proper 'thirties. (Everyone did it then, everyone does it today, but no one *talked* about it then, except in court.)

I'd like to believe the next story, which Roy Hudd swears is true; but I don't. Still, it's well worth telling. Essex police pull up a driver after clocking him doing 95 mph down the motorway.

'Where's the fire?' asks the officer, laconically.

'There's no fire,' says the driver. 'I'm a scriptwriter and I've got to get to Clacton before the matinee to rewrite some comedy material for Roy Hudd.'

'In which case, be on your way,' says the policeman. 'I've seen the show and he needs all the help he can get.'

Diarrhoea – suffered by the driver or the passenger – is occasionally accepted by the police as justification for speeding, presumably on the grounds that a nasty accident could occur if the driver didn't reach a loo in time. Medical emergencies are also given sympathetic consideration in motoring offences – but if it gets to court, you may be asked to produce evidence, such as a letter from the hospital or from your doctor.

I never cease to be amazed by the inventiveness of solicitors or barristers when they come to make their give-my-client-a-break speeches to the court. A solicitor defending a burglar at Kettering, Northamptonshire, told the bench:

'*As you can see, he is going extremely thin on top. He thought people were going to laugh at him.*

'*This had the effect of making him feel unsettled and he went out and committed these offences.*'

The burglar, who admitted three charges and asked for five further offences to be taken into consideration, was given a suspended sentence.

A chap called Wainwright, on the other hand, who murdered his sister-in-law, failed to win the sympathy of the court. When asked why he had done it, he replied: 'Because she had thick ankles.' He was sentenced to death.

The credibility of motorists – and defending lawyers – is frequently stretched to breaking point in drink-driving cases. A 66-year-old major from Whittington, Staffordshire, claimed it was the brandy pudding that pushed him over the top. 'You can hardly cross-examine your hostess about the contents of a dish you are about to eat,' said his defending counsel. The major was fined £45.

TV personality Hughie Green said he was on 'an errand of mercy for a viewer who suffered from asthma' when he was arrested for being unfit to drive through drink. He told Guildford Crown Court:

'As a young man I suffered from asthma but I was cured by a doctor. He later died, but passed on his cure to the doctor who took over the practice. That doctor also eventually died.'

Green explained that an asthma sufferer who watched Opportunity Knocks asked for help, so he drove to see the widow of the second doctor, intending to borrow a medical book. But it could not be found and, during the evening, he had two gins and tonics.

After being stopped by police, Green then failed to blow into a breathalyser. He told the court that this was because he had lost the use of part of a lung.

His complex story was enough to bring tears to the eyes of everyone except the jury and the Recorder. He was fined £250 and banned for three years.

Motorists in danger of losing their licences produce the most fanciful excuses of all, to the constant amusement of the beaks on the bench. But a recent article in *The Magistrate*, the trade paper of the bench, helpfully listed seven 'special reasons' in drink-driving cases which allow magistrates to exercise their discretionary powers *not* to impose a ban.

1 Driving to (but not from) an emergency – i.e., accident to child, fire in shop, there being no other way to contact the emergency services.

2 Unwitting victims of drink-lacing, the victim believing that he is drinking a non-alcoholic drink, or very slightly alcoholic drink.

3 Unwitting and ignorant victim of effect of combination of drugs and small quantity of alcohol.

4 Unwitting exposure to alcoholic fumes in an industrial process.

5 Unwitting victim of electric shock.

6 Unwitting sufferer from disease.

7 Parked vehicle moved a few yards by wedding guest in response to police request.

Take your pick.

For utter finality, you can't beat the excuse, 'I'm dead.' Even the police don't pursue you beyond the grave; unless you're Lord Lucan, that is. A friend – just a friend, you understand – smashed his car up and ended up in hospital for a week with minor head injuries. While there, he was visited by the police who cautioned him, then charged him with dangerous driving, of which he was undoubtedly guilty.

When the summons arrived at his home two or three weeks later, my friend didn't open it but wrote instead on the buff official envelope: '*Addressee deceased as a result of head injuries sustained in motor accident one month ago. Return to sender.*' He then handed the recorded-delivery letter back to the postman. He never heard another word.

In the search for mitigating circumstances, no depth of hypocrisy is too low to stoop to. You can't go far wrong if you remember the words of Abraham Lincoln who once said of a political rival: 'He reminds me of the man who murdered both his parents and then pleaded for mercy on the grounds that he was an orphan.'

POST, lost in the   Contrary to popular belief, the Post Office is not the Bermuda Triangle of delivery services.

'It must have been lost in the post' must therefore be written off as a prospective excuse by every serious failure looking for someone else to blame. I have already outlined elsewhere (**Letters**, failure to answer) the likely causes of letters from other people failing to reach you; I will now advance a couple of explanations as to why your letters may never arrive at their destinations.

1   You didn't have a stamp on you so you put it in the office mail, intending to reimburse the firm later for the cost of postage. Unluckily for you that very day the management decided to stage a series of spot checks to catch out employees sending letters at the firm's expense. Yours was one of the letters intercepted by mail-room security staff and passed on to the deputy managing director to take what action he felt appropriate. Before he could confront you with your crime, he had a heart attack. The file containing the various letters intercepted remained on his desk throughout his long illness, other executives being reluctant to involve themselves in such a sensitive issue. When the deputy managing director died in intensive care two months later, all the letters were quietly shredded to ensure secrecy and avoid a confrontation with the union. You would never have known any of this, but for the fact that your secretary's best friend is having an affair with the

manager of the post room who confided in her the full facts.

2   You put it through the office mail on the day, you now realise, that there was a fire in the post room. A fifteen-year-old acne-scarred messenger girl has since been dismissed on suspicion of arson.

3   You gave it to a normally reliable friend to post who next day flew to America. A good excuse, this, if you then actually write the letter, put it in an envelope, and post it to a friend in America, asking him to post it back from over there. This restores your credibility and may even win you an apology.

4   You posted it while visiting the delightful open-air museum at Beamish, Co. Durham, where, lovingly reconstructed, are Victorian railway stations, turn-of-the-century shops, miners' cottages, and all the memorabilia of yesteryear. The displays included a lovingly restored example of the very first post box in public service, into which you popped your letter, failing to appreciate that it was an exhibit and only an exhibit.

PREARRANGED TELEPHONE CALLS   If you have good reason to suspect that you might be bored to death at a social engagement or a business meeting, then you should plan your early escape in advance with a prearranged telephone call.

It's as easy as saying, 'I have to go.' All you have to do is ask your spouse/secretary/baby-sitter/friend to telephone you at the time you estimate you will be reaching your boredom threshold and to sound suitably grave when asking for you to come to the phone.

When you take the call, you can be confident that everything you say is being listened to with great interest by those present. The key phrases that will get you out of there are as follows:

Is she hurt badly?
Have you called the doctor yet?
Oh, Christ!
Why didn't you call me sooner?
Wait there. I'll be right back.
Of course! Tell the chairman I'm on my way.
How bad is the damage?
*Do everything you can. I'll be with you as soon as I can
    get there.*

You then turn solemnly to your friends or business associates and tell them: 'I'm terribly sorry, but something's cropped up. It's rather important. Will you excuse me? I have to leave at once . . .' With luck you will be out of the building without having to reveal what the imaginary crisis is.

The beauty of this excuse, of course, is that if you are having a perfectly delightful time when the prearranged telephone call comes through, you don't have to leave at all. All you need to be heard saying is, 'I'm having a wonderful time. I thought I told you not to disturb me.'

PRYING, being caught   To the curious, inquiring mind, there is nothing more interesting than the contents of someone else's desk – except, perhaps, the contents of their bedside drawer.

At the same time, being discovered prying into either is about as socially acceptable as being caught with your hand in the till. What were you looking for? Suddenly the curiosity of the person whose privacy you have invaded exceeds even your own.

Your salvation could lie in a box of Kleenex. Most bedside drawers and office desks these days have one. Take two tissues, stuff one up each nostril and lie flat on your back on the floor, explaining that you felt a nosebleed coming on. For greater effect, request a cold, wet flannel. (While your host or hostess are out of the room, you will have time to replace anything your prying may have disturbed.)

Whatever you do, display no signs of your guilt by making any hasty movements. Shut no drawers or cupboard doors. Remember, you are haemorrhaging to death and have nothing to be ashamed of.

If there are no tissues around, then you really are in trouble. The situation is not totally hopeless, however.

Prying in the bedroom

Your embarrassment at discovering your hostess's Aladdin's Cave of sex aids will be impossible to conceal; therefore you must turn it to your advantage. Explain that your piles are killing you and you were mounting a desperate search for a tube of Anusol cream because you were too embarrassed to ask. The obvious place to look, of course, is the very place where you yourself keep such medicaments at home.

Prying in the drawing room

'Isn't that extraordinary?' you remark, having a further poke around the desk, 'my grandmother has a desk that is identical to this one and it has a secret compartment just here. I was looking to see if yours did, too, but it doesn't. Does it have one anywhere else? I'm fascinated by these things . . .'

Prying in the office

What are you looking for in that pile of papers on the managing director's desk?

You are attempting to intercept an ill-considered letter you have written but now wish to withdraw before it is read.

What letter? your inquisitor demands.

'Thank God! Then you haven't received it yet,' you

exclaim, rushing off to continue elsewhere your search for this non-existent epistle.

PUBLIC TRANSPORT Anyone unfortunate enough to be at the mercy of any of our public transport systems is deserving of sympathy, and one could forgive them for murder and arson let alone being twenty minutes late for an appointment.

But for this very reason, in my view, public transport should never be used as an excuse except in special circumstances. It's a cop-out excuse which has become just too handy, and devalued by abuse. Nine out of ten times, you *did* have to wait one hour and ten minutes for a No. 22 bus, but nine out of ten times there will be a lingering suspicion that you spent the one hour and ten minutes in bed and not at a bus stop.

The very fact that public transport is so notoriously unreliable should make it invalid as an excuse. You ought to have known – indeed you did know – that the train would be late, and you should have allowed accordingly for the delay. The inconvenience you have caused others is therefore as much your fault as British Rail's.

Which brings me to those 'special circumstances'. Any delay longer than, say, two hours, could not be foreseen and is permissible as an excuse *provided it is accompanied by the cause* ('Derailment at Doncaster/Baggage handlers' dispute at Orly/Ran aground just off Teneriffe'). But better still are those delays that can be attributed to human failure within the public transport system. Such as the bus driver who loses his way and takes his passengers ten miles off the scheduled route. And the conductor who stops the bus and orders all the passengers off so that he can strip off to locate a wasp that has flown up his regulation-issue trouser leg.

TELEPHONE CALLS, terminating To some telephone junkies, the words 'I really must go now' are a veritable incitement to engage you in conversation for a further forty minutes. In others, they precipitate an attack of verbal diarrhoea. Why won't they take a hint? Why don't they give us a break?

They never will, of course, but getting them off the line without wounding their feelings need be no longer than a thirty-second job.

At home

It's worth having children, if only for the built-in protection they provide from long telephone calls. 'Oh my God, Martha has just fallen downstairs' is all you need to say before replacing the receiver. So is, 'William has just drunk some floor cleaner.' You can't talk to a chatterbox *and* dial 999.

Pets are almost as good. 'I have to rescue my £45 Janet Reger silk cami-knickers from Ben' (Ben being the Great Dane) necessitates replacing the receiver because a long chase may be involved. If you don't have a dog or a cat, you could perhaps report that the budgie has escaped. Or that your neighbour's budgie, free for a fortnight now, has just flown in through the kitchen window.

The question, 'What's the time?' feeds you the line, which ought to be delivered with surprise, that a television programme you *must* watch starts in three minutes.

'There goes the front-door bell' invites the reply, 'I'll hang on while you see who it is,' unless you quickly add: 'It will be the dustmen. I must go, because I want to persuade them to take all the extra rubbish I've left out after the clear-out.' What clear-out? 'Some other time . . .' Click!

A frying pan ablaze on the stove, a smouldering iron face-down on the ironing board, water coming through the ceiling . . . all of these events require your presence elsewhere. More impressive, though, would be an act of good-neighbourliness. 'There's a man with what looks like a jemmy on the roof of the house opposite. I'd better call them immediately just in case he's a burglar and not a workman.'

The callers who chat on tend to be those who telephone most regularly, so you can't keep on experiencing crises every time they ring. The anticipation of an important telephone call ('I must keep the line free . . .') obliges them to ring off. Pretending you can't hear them because of a bad line *your end* is especially effective in stubborn cases.

YOU: Can you hear me all right?
BORE: Yes. As clear as . . .
YOU: What did you say?
BORE (shouting): Yes. I said I can hear you fine.
YOU: I can't hear you, either. Let me call you right back.

You then don't call them back, and when your phone rings three minutes later, you don't answer it. This merely confirms what you have already said, that there is a fault on the line, and you can explain this next time you meet or talk on the phone ('Wasn't it *frustrating*?')

At work

Easy, this, since you can pretend you're working hard. 'I've just had a note put in front of me while we have been talking saying that the manager/foreman has called a meeting which starts in two minutes' time and that I'm expected to attend.'

'Someone is tapping the door. Go away! There seems to be some kind of an emergency. Oh God, they're bleeding. Goodbye.'

TELEPHONING, reasons for not   This actually happened to me, so the excuse comes with my seal of approval, money-back-if-not-satisfied warranty.

'I'm sorry I didn't ring. One of the children snipped through the telephone cable with my wire clippers. I spent more than an hour trying to join up the wires to call you, but without any success. We were in the country, miles from the nearest phone box, and the infuriating thing was, because some people coming to lunch telephoned and heard a ringing tone but got no reply, they assumed we were out and didn't turn up for lunch.'

A less complicated alternative is that you *did* telephone but that there was no reply. This involves a sneaky lie when they reveal that they were in all day and all evening, too. You have to transpose two digits of the telephone number of the person you are supposed to have called and check with them – when they call you, of course – that their number is correctly noted in your book. They then point out that it isn't 3427, it's 3247. An easy mistake, you say.

This is no good for intimates, to whom you have to plead a fault on the line: your phone receives incoming calls but cannot make outgoing calls.

The other day I had a conversation with a business associate which has given me ideas. It went like this:

BUSINESS ASSOCIATE: Why didn't you call me back?
ME: But I returned your call immediately. You weren't in, so I left a message on your answering service.

B.A.: But I don't have an answering service.

ME: This explains why a man I don't know keeps ringing me insisting that I asked him to call me, when I didn't. My call to you must have misrouted. If he calls back, I'll apologise.

TOPICALITY, importance of The more topical your excuse, the more likely it is to be believed. Provided, that is, the excuse isn't Christmas, the miners' strike, or the oil crisis.

Topicality is corroboration. If someone has seen a news report on TV of a ten-mile traffic jam, then they're three-quarters of the way to believing you were stuck in it. If they have read in the papers about a fire that destroyed a dry-cleaner's, they will unquestionably accept that one of the casualties was your dinner jacket without which, at this late hour, you cannot attend the firm's annual dinner-dance tonight.

There is no tragedy, no labour dispute, no event, however small, that cannot provide an alibi for someone wholly unconnected with it. Scan the columns of your local newspaper, sift through the acres of reported affairs in the *Daily Telegraph*. You are sure to find something that will get you off the hook.

TURN UP, failure to So many things, thank goodness, can come between you and an occasion you have promised to attend.

You could, as once happened to a friend of mine, be innocently standing in a telephone box dialling your office when you suddenly find yourself surrounded by five excited police officers who believe that they have at last captured a heavy-breather obscene caller they have been tracking for months.

My friend was invited to make his excuses down at the station while the fingerprints experts set to work. By the time he had convinced them of his innocence, the fingerprint evidence had established it anyway – and the lady had received two more obscene calls in the meantime. Oh yes, and my friend missed a very boring dinner as a result.

'I forgot' is not an excuse that goes down a treat when invitations have been issued and meals prepared. Far better to have remembered but to have suffered the frustration of being inadvertently mortice-locked into your sixth-floor flat by your partner on the very day your telephone was out of order. After unsuccessfully attempting to lower HELP! signs on pieces of string to alert the people in the downstairs flat, you wrote an SOS message, put it in an envelope with a £5 note and tossed it out of the window to a passing stranger. To add insult to injury, he pocketed the money and threw away the note.

Good deeds rate a high forgiveness score in the excuse business. Running over a dog is an immensely time-consuming misfortune guaranteed to make you miss any engagement especially if, in the absence of its owner, you feel obliged to take the wretched animal to a vet who charges you £25 to patch it up. By this time you will have become quite attached to the limping animal in whom you have a financial investment, so you take it back to the scene of the accident in an attempt to find its owner. You enlist the help of the local police and . . .

Getting lost and spending hours looking for the venue is another forgivable reason for not turning up, provided you can give an explorer's horror account of all the places you *did* visit while searching in vain. This requires either a recce of the area or a careful study of the map. An error in noting down the address increases the credibility of this excuse, but you need to refer to the map to find a similar name in the same district to demonstrate the cause of your confusion.

This kind of deception obviously doesn't work with public places, such as hotels or restaurants. Here, your excuse is that while they were waiting for you at the Savoy, you were waiting for them at the Dorchester.

There is also the 24-hour excuse which I stumbled across quite by accident, and in all honesty, when I telephoned some friends to find out if their dinner party that night would be formal or informal.

'Very formal,' said my hostess. 'And it took place *last* night, by the way.'

VISITING, reasons for not I have a phobia about staying in other people's homes and I make no secret of it. If I didn't have a phobia about staying in other people's homes, I would invent one to escape the invitations I ought to accept but would prefer to miss.

Another good excuse for being unable to visit people in their home is that you are working in your own home on a project that requires your day-to-day presence and attention, involving equipment or reference material that is either too great or too numerous to bring with you – such as two hundred reference books or half a ton of marble. Or your own home, possibly. 'I've promised not to accept any invitations away until the place is finished' is an excuse loaded with self-denial.

Not visiting people in hospital calls for a hospital phobia, with which most people would sympathise, or a communicable disease: 'I'd love to come and visit you in hospital, but would you thank me if . . .?'

WEDDING, calling off The best reason for calling off a wedding is the one that is preferably given by telephone from a very great distance. It is: 'Darling, I probably ought to have mentioned this before. I am already married.'

An equally compelling argument against walking up the aisle, or signing the book in the register office, is: 'I don't love you.'

If you want to sugar the pill, however, you could say this:

'When I collected my birth certificate today I discovered that the couple I have called Mum and Dad all my life aren't my real parents at all. My real father was hanged for murder and my real mother was a concentration camp guard who died after the war in an asylum. They never married, so I am also illegitimate. I need some time to think, to discover who I really am now that I know that I'm not the person I thought I was.'

No one will try to talk you out of that one.

WHIP-ROUNDS, not being blackmailed into (*See also* **Charity**, not giving to) The trouble with whip-rounds is that they inevitably become a public scrutiny of how mean or generous you are – when the amount you give is in direct proportion to your affection, esteem, or guilt for the departing colleague.

From time to time, for whatever reason, you will prefer not to contribute so much as one new pee to the farewell present of some odious toadie. Rather than be branded a meanie, all you have to say is: 'I won't contribute to the main present, if you don't mind, because I've bought a little present of my own as a thank you for so many little kindnesses he/she has shown me.' In the euphoria of all the farewell speeches and drinks, no one will discover that you haven't. —

WORK, being late for (*See also* **Oversleeping**) Admiral H. G. Rickover, known in America as 'the father of the nuclear submarine', put this notice on his office door to short-circuit involved excuses from his staff:

To save time for me and yourself, give your excuse by numbers:

1   *I thought I told you.*
2   *That's the way we've always done it.*
3   *No one told me to go ahead.*
4   *I didn't think it was that important.*
5   *I'm so busy I just couldn't get around to it.*
6   *Why bother? The Admiral won't buy it.*
7   *I didn't know you were in a hurry for it.*
8   *That's his job, not mine.*
9   *I forgot.*
10   *I'm waiting for the OK.*
11   *That's not my department.*
12   *How did I know this was different?*
13   *Wait until the boss comes back and ask him.*

Bosses tend to take the same cynical view of excuses advanced by employees who turn up late for work. I must have witnessed several thousands of these, delivered with practised sincerity, but I doubt if more than a handful have been believed. The rule seems to be, the more unlikely the explanation, the more likely it is to be accepted as the truth.

Some years ago a colleague arrived very late for work drenched to the skin. As it was a bright sunny day, clearly two explanations were owed. He told a heart-rending tale of being stuck in an automatic car-wash. His car would neither go forward nor back, and the girl operating the machine didn't know how to switch it off. Finally – so he said, anyway – he had to abandon his car and make a dash for safety through the squirting jets and whirling brushes in an attempt to switch it off himself.

My colleague's heroic escape – as his bad time-keeping had now become – was reported in the following day's newspaper, prompting a reader to write in revealing how he was late for work when his budgie slipped off his bald head into his porridge. It took him ages, he said, to clean the porridge off the bird.

Lloyds Bank house magazine told the story of the cashier who kept on turning up late for work with the explanation: 'I forgot I had been transferred and went to my old branch.'

A friend swears that he overheard the following conversation and that the excuse was believed by the Powers That Be in his office:

EMPLOYEE: *I'm sorry I'm late. Our Alsatian dog mounted my wife while she was drying her hair in front of the fire and pushed her head-first into the grate. I've been at the vet's.*
BOSS: *The vet? Why the vet?*
EMPLOYEE: *My wife hit the dog with a poker and we had to have it put down.*

WRITERS, reasons for not having read their **book** Kingsley Amis says there is only one acceptable excuse for not having read an author's latest book when the author comes to dinner, and it goes like this: '*Your new novel must be absolutely marvellous because I have now bought it three times, and* on every occasion someone has stolen it or borrowed it before I have had a chance to read it. Tomorrow I am going out to buy a fourth copy, and that's going to be MINE.'

Selected Bestsellers

☐ Gone with the Wind	Margaret Mitchell	£2.95p
☐ Robert Morley's Book of Worries	Robert Morley	£1.50p
☐ The Totem	David Morrell	£1.25p
☐ The Alternative Holiday Catalogue	edited by Harriet Peacock	£1.95p
☐ The Pan Book of Card Games	Hubert Phillips	£1.50p
☐ The New Small Garden	C. E. Lucas Phillips	£2.50p
☐ Food for All the Family	Magnus Pyke	£1.50p
☐ Everything Your Doctor Would Tell You If He Had the Time	Claire Rayner	£4.95p
☐ Rage of Angels	Sidney Sheldon	£1.75p
☐ A Town Like Alice	Nevil Shute	£1.50p
☐ Just Off for the Weekend	John Slater	£2.50p
☐ A Falcon Flies	Wilbur Smith	£1.95p
☐ The Deep Well at Noon	Jessica Stirling	£1.75p
☐ The Eighth Dwarf	Ross Thomas	£1.25p
☐ The Music Makers	E. V. Thompson	£1.50p
☐ The Third Wave	Alvin Toffler	£1.95p
☐ Auberon Waugh's Yearbook	Auberon Waugh	£1.95p
☐ The Flier's Handbook		£4.95p

All these books are available at your local bookshop or newsagent, or can be ordered direct from the publisher. Indicate the number of copies required and fill in the form below

3

Name_____
(block letters please)

Address_____

Send to Pan Books (CS Department), Cavaye Place, London SW10 9PG
Please enclose remittance to the value of the cover price plus :

25p for the first book plus 10p per copy for each additional book ordered to a maximum charge of £1.05 to cover postage and packing
Applicable only in the UK

While every effort is made to keep prices low, it is sometimes necessary to increase prices at short notice. Pan Books reserve the right to show on covers and charge new retail prices which may differ from those advertised in the text or elsewhere